LIVING WITHOUT GOD – BEFORE GOD

Living
Without God–Before God

BY DAVID O. WOODYARD

THE WESTMINSTER PRESS · PHILADELPHIA

PUBLISHED BY THE WESTMINSTER PRESS ®
PHILADELPHIA, PENNSYLVANIA

PRINTED IN THE UNITED STATES OF AMERICA

Contents

PART THREE: ASSUMING A CHRISTIAN PERSPECTIVE

Preface

Every generation intent upon doing its believing with sensitivity to the dynamics of its age has a distinctive burden. Our grandparents endured the problem of affirming their faith in a hostile environment. The advances of science appeared to threaten the priorities and the viability of Christianity. In its more primitive and emotive form the issue coalesced around the book of Genesis and Darwin's theory of evolution. Difficult as it is now to recapture the intensity of the "warfare," it was a brutal contest, and the scars from it still mar the contours of the relationship between the scientific and the religious communities. The burden of our parents was that of declaring the faith in all its distinctiveness at a time when everyone was "generally religious." For the gospel to get a hearing amid "the noise of solemn assemblies" was a task of no mean proportion. Christianity has historically been least effective when it was "in." To maintain the "rough edges" of faith in a politely pious ethos constituted their burden. Now, for the third generation the conflict with science lies dormant, and the popularity of religion has been replaced by indifference. Our unique burden appeared at first to be merely a matter of securing modern words for an ancient tradition. We gravitated to

Professors Bultmann and Tillich for guidance in translation. Without them many of us would have been dropouts
a decade ago. But it is becoming increasingly clear to
some of us that the problem is not converting the words
of antiquity into those of the "jet age" but those realities
to which the words themselves point. While we began
groping for a new vocabulary, we are now unsure about
the experiences they articulate. This, in the final analysis,
is the significance of the "death of God" theologies. Their
precise claims about God are difficult to accept; how can
mortals know that kind of data about the divine? But
these radical theologies have forced many of us to acknowledge that there is a "missing referent" in much of
our believing. We need to relocate in our own experience
what the words of faith, old and new, are defining.

These chapters are no more than one Christian's attempt to do his believing while aware of this problem.
The first part deals specifically with the problem of
transcendence, where we experience it and how we can
express it. The second part deals with the broader range
of claims and practices within the Christian community
and how they might be interpreted. The final part ex-
amines in the perspective of faith certain issues that are
defined for us by our age. One might note the absence
of a chapter on the church. That could reflect a negative
frame of mind on its possibilities, but it could also serve
as a testimony that the church is everywhere present as
that locus within which man does his believing.

Chapter 3: "The Absence of God," Chapter 10: "The
Hell of Hell," Chapter 12: "Isn't One Religion as Good
as Another?" and Chapter 13: "Away with the Manger"
are adapted from sermons that appeared originally in *The
Pulpit*, copyright 1962, 1966, 1963, and 1965 by The
Christian Century Foundation. They are reprinted, by

permission, from the June 1962, January 1966, July-August 1963, and December 1965 issues of *The Pulpit*. Chapter 18: "The Neighbor Is a Negro," is being published as a sermon in *Best Sermons*, edited by George Paul Butler, published by Trident Press, March, 1968.

In the creation of a book an author has no one to blame and many to thank. My secretary, Mrs. Burton Dunfield, not only has typed and retyped these pages but has compensated for my inability to spell. Her high level of competence has saved me countless hours. Sara Jane, age six, and Kimberly Ann, age four, provided several illustrations and many distractions. My wife, Joanne, endured the manic-depressive behavior that dominated the days of writing. My father, mother, and sister first exposed me to the love which makes faith credible. This book is dedicated to Dr. Paul Scherer, the kind of teacher who stands by a man's side the rest of his life—even when he cannot side with the contours of his student's thought.

D. O. W.

PART ONE

SPEAKING OF GOD AND CHRIST

1

The Ominous Hollow Noun

This is not the first generation that has presumed to declare the death of God. The claim reaches back to Nietzsche in the nineteenth century and has Hegel for an ancestor of sorts. But the obituary now being published is unique in that those who have written it choose to maintain their identity as Christians. Prof. William Hamilton, formerly of Colgate Rochester Divinity School, makes it quite clear that he is concerned both with the "death of God" and with the Lordship of Christ in the world. What he understands as obedience to Jesus precludes casting his lot either with traditional atheism or with pure humanism.

It is not easy to grasp with clarity what the radical theologians are advocating with the "death of God" slogan. That in part is related to a dearth of lucidity in their writings and to divergent trends within the movement. But it is also a function of our temptation to deflect their message by identifying it with some familiar cate-

gory. Perhaps we can approach an understanding by dis-
claimer. They are not saying with the typical atheist that
there never has been a God and men ought be honest
enough to admit it. They are not saying with some ex-
istentialists that God is absent and the void is the form
of his presence. They are not saying with Harvey Cox
that the word "God" needs to be set aside until a new
image appears with which we may speak of him. And
they are not saying with Dietrich Bonhoeffer that certain
concepts of God must be abstracted from the vocabulary
of faith. Profs. William Hamilton and Thomas J. J.
Altizer specify the central thrust of the radical theology
as follows: "There once was a God to whom adoration,
praise and trust were appropriate, possible, and even
necessary, but . . . now there is no such God."[1] Something happened to God. That is the nub of the argument.

Some have responded to this thesis with an intricate
analysis of its validity, some with a violent torrent of
emotion, and others with stony indifference. I propose
now to respond on another level, one that sidesteps the
burden of evaluation, and explore several points at which
their claims touch our experience and awaken the possibilities of a faithful life.

I

For one thing, they have identified the difficulty that
many of us have in speaking the words of the Christian
tradition, particularly the word "God." The novelist John
Updike refers to the divine name as "the ominous hollow
noun." At times one wonders if it will ever again mean anything to us. The Biblical writers seem so sure of who God
is, where God is, and what he has done. They describe him
as Love, they place him in heaven, and they claim certain

events as his action in history. But these references are
meaningless to men who take seriously the world in which
they live. For many, God seems unrelated to their experiences and their knowledge. And I for one am finding
myself increasingly embarrassed and repelled by those
who invoke the divine name with ease. I feel squeamish
when someone is reflecting upon his anticipations of
tomorrow and adds the phrase "God willing." It strikes
me as dishonest when a politician extols how God has
blessed this great country with prosperity. And when
someone refers to God as his "constant companion" in
life, it all seems a bit naïve.

The trouble is that we have been putting the divine
name in all the wrong places—where there was a mystery
we could not penetrate, where there was a need to be
fulfilled, where there was an emotion to be controlled.
For modern man the word "God" no longer sticks in
these places. It has been dislodged by our expanding
knowledge and social programs. Science dispels the
mysteries, psychiatry manages the emotions, and the
government provides for our needs.

This leads me to confess that there are some dead gods
and to rejoice in the funeral orations. The God who
created the universe in six days and rested on the seventh
like a good union man, that God is dead. The God who
controls our lives until our freedom is a farce, that God
is dead. The God who inflicts suffering and death as
retribution for sin, that God is dead. The God who des-
tines some men for heaven and others for hell, that God
is dead. The God who calls men out of the world for
spiritual experiences, that God is dead. The God who
makes us think less of ourselves to see our need of him,
that God is dead. The God who causes some men to die
and allows others to live, that God is dead. And thank

God for that! These are corpses masquerading as divinity, and it is time for a burial.

In saying this, we have not resolved the difficulty in speaking the words of faith. But if from the radical theologians we can learn to stop pasting the divine name in the wrong places, by the grace of God we may begin to fix it in some of the right ones.

II

A second theme that we can appropriate from these radical theologians is their affirmation of the world. They are challenging us to recognize its essential goodness and to embrace all it can do for us. Prof. William Hamilton makes the point compellingly: "We do not ask God to do for us what the world is qualified to do. . . . We trust the world, not God, to be our need fulfiller and problem solver."[2] There's really nothing new being said here. What the "death of God" theologians are doing is to take seriously the creation myth. There God stood back, looked at his handiwork, and said, "It is good, it is very good."

But Christians have seldom accepted that endorsement of the world. The usual implication is that the worldly realities are to be suspected, if not degraded. What matters for faith is some spiritual realm where all is as it should be. The secular and the demonic are often equated. We have heard it said that a man with real faith would never have to see a psychiatrist. We have been led to believe that what counts in marriage is love and that sex is the dirty dimension of it. And we have been told that a man's possessions are somehow evil and that he ought to be free of them as though poverty were a virtue.

Against all this the radical theologians are calling upon

us to trust the world and the way it is dealing with its own problems. There is no reason to believe that God need take care of it or that when the world does the job, faith is threatened. And we ought not to miss the significance of this joyful acceptance of the world and its processes. Certainly it saves us from the inclination long bred and still nourished in the Christian community to perceive every discovery of science as an inherent challenge to faith. Trusting the goodness of the world frees us to embrace them without guilt or reservation. Nothing is evil until man makes it so by the manner in which he uses it. This affirmation of the worldly ought also to enable us to respond creatively to the processes of urbanization and technology. While some would see the movement from the pastoral and more primitive as a disaster, those who take seriously the goodness of creation can perceive them as occasions for new forms and dimensions of humanization. One need not be disturbed by the inability to relate God to the subways as one did to the soil or one's Christian style to a room full of IBM machines as one did to the small business in the backyard. The absence of a religious reference or solution is not a cause for wailing. Then one might also call attention to the secular world's taking responsibility for providing schools, hospitals, and mental institutions—tasks once performed by the church. Some would argue that only a "God-fearing man" can really heal or teach the truth. But the facts are often almost the opposite in many instances. The world has learned to be its own problem solver and need fulfiller; it has come of age. That this should happen without any reference to divinity, or even in apparent denial, is a cause for rejoicing. God declared the world to be good and it ill behooves us to do less.

Thus the radical theologians would elicit from us a

faithful respect for the world's maturation and independence. We need not look to God for what the world can do for us. The curious paradox these theologians have drawn into focus for us is this: one's true faithfulness is in inverse relation to one's reliance upon the God hypothesis and in direct relation to one's trusting the world's ability to meet its own problems.

III

I have been suggesting two things of significance for us in the "death of God" theology. The first is that these theologians are teaching us to withdraw the divine name from the wrong places where we have put it. And secondly, by doing that, they are enabling us to accept the glory and integrity of our worldly life. But this does not mean we are set adrift in the world with no claims upon us. Listen again to Dr. Hamilton: "I insist that the time of the death of God is also the time of obedience to Jesus. . . . [He is] a figure of sufficient clarity . . . [to be for us the] center for Christian faith and life. . . . Jesus is the one . . . before whom I stand, the one whose way with others is also to be my way. . . . I am drawn, and I have given my allegiance."[3]

On first hearing, that may sound like the traditional piety, and you can chalk it up to that if you choose. But I find here a clue to the shaping and styling of an authentically human life. I don't consider myself a Christian because I embrace certain creeds; they often confuse and confound until faith itself is dried up. I don't consider myself a Christian because I worship on Sundays; churches often seem more like tombs than temples. But I do struggle with being a Christian in joy and humility because in the event of Jesus Christ I find the depth and breadth of what it means to be a human being. And I find it nowhere else with the same clarity and contagion. What this event of words and deeds does is to provide me with an image of what my life is called to be. Jesus for me is not an article in a tattered creed, but a way to be in the world. By standing against me in all the imperfections of my being, he stands for the man I could become.

What I mean to suggest is that he gets in the way of my being a lesser self, of falling short of the very humanness I could achieve. He stands against my impulse to hate another who has offended me and challenges me to accept in another the defects I tolerate in myself. He stands against my indifference to the plight of others and challenges me to confirm their goodness and sustain their dignity. He stands against my desire to possess everything for myself and challenges me to share my abundance with others. He stands against my unruly love of self and challenges me to love my neighbor with the same ardor. I have given my allegiance to him because he is forever calling forth a depth and breadth of humanness in a way no one else can. And from time to time in his claim upon my life I recognize more than the action of a man. I must confess to seeing "the glory of God in the face of Christ" (II Cor. 4:6).

2

The Name Will Come Later

There is often a feeling of embarrassment when in our presence someone mentions God. Even reading the word now may provoke uneasiness. Revulsion at emotional expressions of piety and distortions of the faith are at least in part the reason. Yet another, less personal but perhaps more significant, suggests itself: There is no consensus on the meaning of the word; it does not order our thoughts and feelings into decisive form. It used to be said that there is a "God-shaped blank" in the consciousness of man, a gap only a divine could fill. Now it might be said that in the consciousness of man there is a "blank-shaped God"; the multiplicity of meanings that have clustered around the divine name make its impact indistinct. The problem is sufficiently intense for some theologians to propose a moratorium on the word: that we strike it from our vocabulary until we can reclaim it with precision.

Now for different reasons an event in the Old Testament centers on the divine name. While Moses is tending his father-in-law's sheep in the desert, he hears a voice that commands him to lead his people out of bondage. Anxious about the identity of the One who speaks to him, he asks, "What is your name?" That's natural enough; we would do as much. But the answer is disappointing, if not disturbing: "I am who I am." God responds to Moses by withholding his name.

I

We shall forever miss the significance of this dialogue until we ask why the name was so important to Moses. For our part, we couldn't care less. It's little more than a convenient label by which to distinguish one person from another. But in the ancient Near East a name is a sacred thing, for it is identical with the very essence of a person. The substance of one's selfhood is disclosed in the name to which he answers. In The First Book of Samuel it is said of Nabal, "as his name is, so is he" (I Sam. 25:25); Nabal literally means "fool." So what Moses is really asking of God is this: Tell me who you really are, share the inner secrets of your being, that my people and I may trust you. An echo of that is in a demand once made upon me by a student: "Just tell me who God is and I will believe in him."

But what Scripture reveals is that the one thing we will never know is who God is; at best, he gives only intimations of his nature. What I dread most as a father is the day when my little daughters will ask me to explain God to them. I can't tell them who he is. No one can. When God says to Moses, "I am who I am" (Ex. 3:14), he is saying, "You'll have to go along without my name, without knowing my identity." Old Testament scholar Martin Noth has come as close as anyone to the meaning of the passage when he paraphrases it: "I am something, but it will turn out what I am."[4] To know God you have to wait; and even then you will never know him, not really.

Perhaps this is precisely what we in our time and place

need to hear: You not only cannot know God, you should
not claim to. That may sound like the antithesis of a
faithful word, but it is in fact the possibility of faithfulness. The less you claim to know about God, the better
is your chance of knowing him. The message of the
Scripture passage is this: Travel light, religiously travel
very light. That's the measure of your faith. Hold as few
images and conceptualizations as you can and still stand
fast; cling to as few moral demands as you can and still
be true; identify as few perceptions of his will as you can
and still be sensitive to his leading. This is not because
God is himself in the process of becoming as some
theologians suggest, but because you must always be in
the process of becoming aware of who God is. In the
mind of man a god defined is a god denied. Hiddenness
and mystery are intrinsic to the divine nature. He is
always more than you can gather into an image or a
concept. The beginning and the end of faith is to say, "I
do not know God." That is not a counsel of despair but
an affirmation of his nature. Often the most we can say
about him is a confession of how little we can know about
him. Our knowledge of him comes in bits and pieces.

II

This leads to a second meaning in the response to
Moses. "I am who I am" can as well be translated, "I
cause to be what I cause to be." That interpretation is
confirmed in the term "Yahweh" so common in the Old
Testament. It is derived from the Hebrew word "to be"
and identifies God as the one who causes things to be. For
the Bible the question is never *if* God is, it is seldom *who*
God is, it is always *where* God is. And the answer re-

sounds: God is where things are happening. In the words
of a soft-drink ad, he is "where the action is."

Our inclination is to confine him to some sacred place,
some temple where we can turn for refuge. That is why
Moses was taken off guard when he came upon God in
the desert. He had thought God was back in Palestine
where he belonged. But the Lord confronted him, saying,
"Put off your shoes from your feet, for the place on
which you are standing is holy ground." In other words,
"Right where you are is where God is, . . . the immediate
situation is the only holy ground you'll ever know."[5]

Several summers ago some ministers in Chicago prepared an experimental liturgy for an ecclesiastical gathering. Its purpose was to suggest in worship the presence of
God in the wanton shriek and despicable agony of city
life. Contention over its validity has emerged. The lines
that most people seek out for censure are these: "O God,
who is all men; O God, who smells and has no place to
bathe; O God, who hangs on street corners, who tastes the
grace of cheap wine and the sting of the needle." At other
points the liturgy continues, "O God, whose name is
Spick, black nigger, bastard, guinea, and kike." *The
Christian Century* called it "unintentionally blasphemous."
And in a way it is; any simple equation of God and man
is a distortion. But it's the kind of blasphemy in which
the Bible itself participates. It represents a reckless and
foolish deity who does not confine himself to some
celestial palace but involves himself in the rigors and
ruptures of human life. God is where the action is; where
you are is holy ground.

He is where the bigotry and immaturity of some is met
by the passion for justice of others; he's in the struggle
of a man and woman to find the fulfillment of their lives

in marriage; he's where men attempt to be whole and human in their dealings with one another; he's in the protests men erect against the structures of society that warp lives and distort personalities; he's where men gather themselves in communities and seek the meaning of brotherhood. I make bold to suggest it's not God's way to be present in religious calisthenics where men pride themselves on their piety. God is where the action is, where things are happening. And as you participate in what he's doing, you'll begin to know who he is. When you lay hold of life, its source lays hold of you.

III

Two things have been said about the dialogue between God and Moses. The first is that you'll never know God or grasp any definitive image of his nature. He withholds his name. The mark of your faithfulness is the courage to engage life without his identity in full view. And the second is that although you can never know who God is, you can know where God is. He's where you are, where things are happening to you and around you. That's the only holy ground you'll ever know.

But at this point the Old Testament reaches out for the New. In the book of John, Jesus is reported to have said in a prayer, "I made known to them thy name, and I will make it known, that the love with which thou hast loved me may be in them" (John 17:26). That might appear to contradict what was said to Moses, but it is as well the fulfillment of a promise given to him. I hope you have in mind the paraphrase of Martin Noth: "I am something, but it will turn out what I am." And it does; as much as we can handle of that is given in Jesus Christ even as it remains hidden "in the stable of human history."

But we shall do violence to this event if we allow ourselves to think about it in categories of human and divine and how they can be conjoined. Jesus calls no attention to himself as a figure with which to reckon. But he does point by word and deed to what is happening through him. And it's this which makes him the one through whom the divine name can be known. With no craving for divinity himself, he can be transparent to the mystery he reveals. His only mission is to incarnate in the presence of men the love with which he is loved and make its reality felt.

That's why contemporary theologians call him "the man for other men." He's the one in whom Love has completely taken over—in whom it is revealed that the depth and ground of all our being is love. With no need to protect his dignity or flash his credentials he could accept those whom others rejected, forgive those others held in guilt, and care for those whose needs others ignored. In the way he was with men, he became the image and reflection of his father.

I've wrestled for years with how I could grow in that and share its meaning with others. More times than not, frustration has created new frustrations. The brutal fact is that none of us can deliver Christ to another. But we can identify moments in which we have experienced his love even if we could not call it by its proper name. If you have known a moment in which another person has touched you deeply with some disclosure of himself and found yourself free to do the same, if you have known a moment in which you wounded another by word or deed but from the depths of his hurt the response was forgiveness, if you have known a moment in which your most desperate need for compassion and understanding was met by another's willingness to give it, or if you have known a moment in which the task before you seemed beyond your fulfillment but were given the strength to persevere—then you have known the love with which Christ was loved. Do not be disturbed if you cannot identify it with the divine name. Accept the gift and live in the power of it. The name will come later.

3

The Absence of God

When a playwright and a philosopher hold up a mirror in which we see the same reflection of our experience, we ought to view it with some seriousness. The image they project is that of men tormented and frustrated by the absence of God. Tennessee Williams confronts us with it in *Sweet Bird of Youth*. Through the heckler he says, "I believe that the long silence of God, the absolute speechlessness of Him, is a long, long, and awful thing that the world is lost because of. . . ."[6] And German existentialist Martin Heidegger directs us to the same experience. "I do not deny God," he writes, "I state his absence. . . . Here is the problem of our world."[7]

Lest we think this the nonsense of godless men and priests of despair, let the record be set straight: While the Bible does witness to those moments in which men experienced God's presence, it is equally careful to report those in which men experienced his absence. There's that floundering band of Israelites bemoaning the fact that there were no prophets (II Kings 3:11) in their midst as assurances of God's direction; there's the psalmist with his cry centuries later to be echoed from a cross, "My God, my God, why hast thou forsaken me?" (Ps. 22:1);

and there's Job pleading, "Oh, that I knew where I might find him" (Job 23:3).

We are not alone in our feeling that God has withheld his presence. His absence has hovered over the lives of men like a thundercloud that threatens but never yields rain. And so we wait, frustrated by failure and tortured by guilt. What are we to make of this? How are we to understand what is happening to us?

I

Certainly one thing that causes us to experience God's absence is the misconception we hold of his presence. The form in which we expect him is not always the manner in which he comes. This was the tragic flaw in the expectations of the Jews of the first century. They had expected a Messiah robed in glory and possessed of power. But when Jesus lay in a manger and hung on a cross, they could not see in him the presence of God.

This is a theme which Samuel Beckett develops in his play *Waiting for Godot*—waiting for God, if you will have it that way. Through the drama two hoboes wait for a mysterious figure who has promised to come to them. They are vague as to what he is like and even who he is. But their image of him is surely dramatic and spectacular. His coming will be no ordinary event. As the curtain falls on the last act, nothing has happened. They have whiled away eventless time, considered suicide as a release from boredom, and thought of giving up waiting and hoping.

The tragedy in the play is not that Godot did not come but that he came and they failed to recognize him. There had been an interruption in their idle routine of which they made nothing. Pozzo entered with his slave, Lucky, on a rope. Pozzo treats this man like a dog—teasing him, striking his side, withholding love and affection. In one production of the play, the director had Lucky angle toward the barren tree on the stage and make as if it were a cross. But the two hoboes missed it all. They were waiting for Godot and could not be bothered with this nonsense. Well, the nonsense was Godot! And they missed him for all their conceptions of what his presence would be like.

If nothing else, this parable reflects the absence of God which modern man experiences. We yearn for nothing so much as his presence. But he comes and goes and we never know it for all the limits we put on the manner he is to be with us.

We expect him in a dramatic event that bespeaks his power and dignity, but he comes in the humiliation that is the measure of his love. We expect him to shout forth from the heavens with an angry voice at the ways of men, but he judges with stony silence. We expect him to grasp us at worship, but he stalks the lonely pathways of main street in the deepest need of a person. We expect him while on our knees at prayer, but he appears when we stand erect and confident before a challenge. We expect him at eventide as the sun sets and the dusk embraces the landscape, but he comes in the freshness of each day's opportunity. We expect him to stand in our midst as some cosmic ghost, but he invades the life of a man until he images his Creator.

God is not absent; it's just that we are blind to the mysterious and ordinary ways in which he comes to us. "The life of every man," writes Alan Richardson, "is full of pieces of unrecognized knowledge of God, intimations of the divine presence which most people never learn to call by their proper names."[8] Perchance, someday we will associate the experience and the name and recognize the events for what they really are—instruments of God's presence in a world that bemoans his absence.

II

Now, secondly, what we believe to be his absence may really be the form of his presence. Scripture is unmistakably clear that God is always hidden when he reveals himself. He is not one whom we can draw into the range of our vision or the realm of our touch. "Truly," said the prophet Isaiah, "thou art a God who hidest thyself." (Isa. 45:15.) Anything other than that is not the God of the Biblical faith.

There was a day when Moses demanded that God stand before him and lay bare his nature to scrutiny: "I pray thee, show me thy glory." And God replied: "I will make all my goodness pass before you . . . ; I will be gracious to whom I will be gracious, and will show mercy on whom I will show mercy. But . . . you cannot see my face; for man shall not see me and live. . . . Behold, there is a place by me where you shall stand upon the rock; and while my glory passes by I will put you in a cleft of the rock, and I will cover you with my hand until I have passed by; then I will take away my hand, and you shall see my back; but my face shall not be seen." (Ex. 33:18-23.) We have to do with a God who is hidden when he is revealed. How else are we to understand the event of Christ? For all the world he appeared to be no more than a man. Yet really for all the world God was there in him. Nothing seems less likely than that he should take on the form of a man unless one had come to understand the determination of this God to be with man! Men who have come to know God were found

by him at the very point they would never think of
looking!

So in those moments when we feel most keenly his
absence, we should be most alert to his presence. God
is never directly discernible but comes to us "in, with, and
under" ordinary events. There is always some medium
charged with his presence and struggling to make known
his will.

He may be in a personal crisis when despair outdis-
tances hope; he may be in a relationship when person
faces person free of defenses; he may be in that struggle
for independence from parents when determination is
bound by guilt; he may be in a romance when the chords
of love are struck for the first time; he may be in the
injustices of life when we find ourselves outraged that
he permits them; he may be in the frustrated efforts to
find him when we imagine we are forsaken.

God is never so present as when everything argues for
his absence. That was the experience of Dietrich Bonhoeffer. Imprisoned by the Nazis, deprived of the presence
of those he loved, restrained from performing his function
as minister, he wrote from his lonely cell: "I'm sure
everything that happens to me has a purpose, even if it
cuts across my own wishes. As I see it, I am here [in
prison] for a purpose, and I only hope I am living up to
it."[9] In his hour of darkness when outward events bespoke
God's absence, by faith he discerned God's presence.

That's the task to which we are set when we feel as
though God has left us and our world to wind its own
way into destruction: not bemoaning a cruel desertion,
but alerting ourselves to the guises "in, with, and under"
which he comes to us. We shall never see him face-to-face.
His presence is always mediated through events and rela-

tionships. We can know God only when we accept the fact that he is always hidden as he reveals himself.

III

One thing more—the hiddenness of God which we experience as his absence is the way he sustains our freedom and responsibility. God puts limits upon himself, bridles his power, that we might be men and not pawns. Over the created order he has given *us* dominion.

Yet a look at our world seems to dictate something else. That a funny little man in the Kremlin can hold events so tightly in his greedy fists, that an Eichmann can bear within him such bestiality and feel no remorse, that a white man can so righteously limit and abuse another because of his color, would seem to signal an abdication of power. "What strikes the mind so forcefully and painfully," wrote John Henry Newman, "is his absence from his own world. . . . It's as if others had got possession of his work."[10]

It was a terrible risk God took—and once upon a time it cost him his Son. Yet he has never repented of it. Anything less than that would be to make us less than human. We can go a long way before we come up against a boundary and know we have reached the limit of God's patience and our freedom.

All that some can see in this is withdrawal and desertion. Yet the Biblical faith sees this hiddenness as God's way of giving us responsibility. Thus W. H. Auden writes: "Our dominant experience [today] is of God's absence, of His distance. . . . For our time, the distance of God may be something He wishes us to learn."[11] It is his way of saying: "Come on now, man, this world is in your hands. Make something of it."

No futile gesture, that. You cannot view a Rembrandt painting, watch a Shakespearean play, listen to a Bach oratorio, observe the United Nations struggle with justice, benefit from the discoveries of science, witness the response of college students to the Peace Corps, and feel that it was not worth the gamble—and the heartache. Man is not the "eternal sophomore" Wallace Stevens claims him to be.

When we begin to think that God has withdrawn himself from our midst, it is time to realize that this is a silence which speaks. Make no mistake about what it says: This is a world in which you have freedom and responsibility. You can make of it a hell on earth for yourself and others or a world that reflects the God who created it. Human relationships can be warm and meaningful or they can be empty and frustrating. Learning can be a retreat from life and responsibility or it can be a preparation for assuming one's work. Life itself can be "one long headache on an empty street" or it can have the meaning God intended for it. By keeping hidden, God leaves it up to us. It's not that he's lost interest and washed his hands of it; it's that he thinks our hands are worthy of the trust. More than once we have given him reason to believe this isn't so; yet never has he been tempted to have it otherwise.

We began with a glance in the mirror that a playwright and a philosopher hold up to us. They touch a live nerve with their image of us as plagued by the absence of God. But now, perhaps, we see that this absence is the manner of his presence. If not today, then some other day, our cry with Job, "Oh, that I knew where I might find him" (Job 23:3), will be transformed into the discovery of Jacob at Bethel, "Surely the LORD is in this place; and I did not know it" (Gen. 28:16).

4

The Claim to Be and a Way to Be

Recently I was interrogated by a religious superpatriot who felt called upon to assess my orthodoxy. The experience was like being set upon by the FBI, the CIA, and the John Birch Society—all at once. I flunked! That became apparent when he turned on me and said, "The trouble with you, David, is that you are embarrassed by the word 'God.' " Now that's a bum rap for a preacher! But I have to admit that he is right—for reasons, however, he could neither understand nor appreciate. The embarrassment centers on having a word the content of which has evaporated, a word that no longer connects with experience. Using the divine name is rather like taking a swing at a punching bag only to find upon contact that someone has let the air out of it.

Another way of saying this is that many of the conventional ways in which we have referred to God are no longer viable. There was a time when many of us could discourse on the divine nature with a string of adjectives; but a generation, for example, that no longer experiences awe and wonder has no content for a word like "holy." There was a time in which many of us could conceive of God as that for which man innately longed; but this inclination to reach out or up for a beyond has abated.

There was a time in which many of us used God as an explanation for things we could not otherwise understand; but now we live more comfortably with ignorance, waiting for science to fill the gaps. And there was a time in which we turned to God as a refuge from the blunders of existence; now we are more apt to seek comfort in a gracious neighbor. For many of us the divine name drifts over our experience without making contact.

It might appear on the surface that this contention is an echo of what several of the radical theologians are arguing. Certainly all of us who are concerned with theology are indebted to them not only for focusing upon the central problem of faith but for holding up to us the vacuity of our transcendent references. Yet I must disassociate myself from their position on two counts—crucial ones, I think. First, while they are dealing with an event in the life of God, I am concerned with an event in the consciousness of man. Thomas J. J. Altizer maintains that God died in the first century, on the cross, in the person of Jesus. William Hamilton argues that the death occurred sometime in the nineteenth century and is taking its written records under scrutiny to determine when. In an earnest effort to avoid subjectivism they are compelled to locate something that happened to God and to which we are responding. Richard Rubenstein, in his own Jewish tradition a radical, protests quite properly: "No man can really say that God is dead. How can we know that? . . . This is more a statement about man and his culture than about God."[12] It would appear to be more reasonable to maintain that we are no longer able to live the symbols once identified with the divine.

Then there is another distinction: While the radical theologians and Hamilton in particular are engaged in an experiment to see if they can make it as Christians without God, I am interested in an experiment to see if we can make it as Christians with God. It might seem that their project is more daring and adventuresome. Perhaps it is, but that is not relevant to its validity. I find the burden of the modern Christian defined more meaningfully by the patron saint of the radical theologians, Dietrich Bonhoeffer, who contended that we must live in the world without God yet before him. Bonhoeffer was searching for a style that affirmed God as God but refused to use him as a means of getting along in the world. For me the real excitement is in struggling to find a way of speaking about this God. And the test of strength is to stand by the claim that there is something in me but not of me, even though our symbols and images for that have fossilized.

In order to do this we must suspend for now our traditional assertions about the divine. It is incumbent upon us to recognize that the claims that God is holy, that Jesus is divine, and that the Holy Spirit is mysterious no longer define anything with which we are familiar. The time may come when we can once again stand within the secure womb of tradition and give expression to our faith in conventional ways—but it will only be after we have identified in our experiences some realities with which to link them. Let me now relate my attempt to link the divine name with things I know to be real in my existence.

I

I begin with an experience of up-againstness. While I attempt to live my life for my own benefit and on my own terms, I continually encounter a claim upon my being, a *claim to be,* which is not part of my inner equipment or simply the stimulants in my environment. I can best express it as the realization that I am not entirely my own man, that I am obligated from beyond myself and others—though in the midst of both. As I attempt to live self-consciously I am aware of demands and boundaries that preclude simply letting go of myself. When you take your existence as a unique person seriously and do not try to escape the radical demands that your being makes upon you, you know that it is not your own to do with as you please. There is a claim to be that you neither can generate nor control, a demand you can tranquilize but not abort. To be truly alive is to know you are up against something claiming you for what you alone can be.

Let me see now if I can be more specific and identify situations in which this may happen. It may be at a moment in which you are tempted to compromise yourself and cheat the future of its possibilities; it may be at a moment when you have an impulse to hurt someone who has wounded you; it may be at a moment in which you want to give up some discipline and relax into a flabby mode of existence; or it may be at a moment in which you see nothing worthwhile to do. But in the midst of these moments you experience something backing up against the inclination to give in and give up. The temptation to compromise is met by a claim for integrity, the impulse to hurt is met by the possibility of compassion, the disenchantment with discipline is met by the necessity for it, and the meaninglessness is met by a task you feel called to do.

Now I identify God with these experiences of up-againstness. I am as aware as you that other names can be used and that the experiences themselves can be explained away. But for me, and I would argue for the

Biblical writers as well, these are moments when the divine is in the midst of our lives staking out a claim. In the words of Harvey Cox: "We met God at those places where we are both stopped and challenged. . . . God meets us . . . at those aspects of our experience which can never be transmuted into extensions of ourselves."[13] I associate God with those moments when I am up against something which claims me for the man I could be. You may call it something else; ultimately what matters is that we respond to the claim and live up to it.

II

But now I want to go on and express my conviction that up-againstness, the claim to be, has content as well as form. For me the nature of my obligation has the shape of an event in the first century. Yet I find this a difficult event about which to speak. There is something obscene about the mode and manner in which many Christians refer to Christ. The game of many who play with human and divine categories and how they can be fitted together is often a cruel hoax. The image of a sexless saint generated by a precious picture of Jesus over the altar in a pink sanctuary is grotesque. The radio broadcasts on Sunday mornings with their sweet talk about gentle Jesus coming into your heart borders on perversion. What comes of these references is sentimentality at best and distortion at worst.

Now that I have made these ungracious remarks, it is incumbent upon me to expose my own perceptions for your evaluation. When I make reference to Christ I am talking about a *way to be,* that there was an event in history from which I have learned and am learning to style my life in history. Christ represents both the possibilities of my existence and the claim to engage them. He holds against me in an utterly contagious way an image of the human being I could be. In the words of the late Robert Spike, I am "disturbed and intrigued"[14] by what I see in Christ. To settle for anything less than that is as repellent as ten cents' worth of cold coffee.

Specifically, this event claims me for the possibility that I can be relevant to my environment without being a carbon copy of its expectations; that I can risk the sneers and laughter of some because I am responsible to another image of acceptability; that I can take upon myself the hurts and humiliations of others in the conviction that this is the kind of man I am called to be; that I can be confident about the possibilities of the future in the assurance that the past is not my destiny; that I can trust myself as a good thing whether or not I receive the confirmation of certain people. I am "disturbed and intrigued" by what I see in Christ because what I see is the human being I am called to be.

Now, do you see my argument? I have found in my experience a *claim to be,* up-againstness, and a *way to be,* Christ. When these two meet, I can use the word "God."

5

Denying What One Cannot Endure

There can be little doubt that for many in our time the sense of intimacy with God has ebbed, if not dried up entirely. Where faith remains, it is evident more in form than in substance. Few are so bold as to deny that there is a supreme being somewhere "who got it all going." Many stand by the church as "a force for good in the community" and pay their dues like responsible citizens. And then a goodly number find much to be admired in Jesus; "He is probably the best man that ever lived," they say. Yet the overriding sense that there is a God for me, with me, and against me loses out before the telling tribunal of experience. Reluctant as they are to admit it, many are awakening to the fact that God means nothing to them anymore. They did not want it that way; but now it is that way, and they must make the best of it. The habit of "getting along without God" perpetuates itself effortlessly, and we often feel no worse for it. And as if to assure himself that he can make it through the freaks of fate with some hope of survival, modern man embraces his neighbor as the source of salvation. That is the way it works out in Archibald MacLeish's *J.B.*, a rather contorted modern Job. Sarah and J.B. have gone through all the modern equivalents of Job's agony:

One daughter raped and murdered by an idiot,
Another crushed by stones, a son
Destroyed by some fool officer's stupidity,
Two children smeared across a road
At midnight by a drunken child—[15]

Sarah has left J.B. and returned. In the final moments of
the play she holds his head in her hands and says:

Blow on the coal of the heart.
The candles in churches are out.
The lights have gone out in the sky.
Blow on the coal of the heart
And we'll see by and by . . .[16]

As the curtain falls, one is aware of two human beings
clinging desperately to the compassion they have for each
other. The sense of intimacy with anything ultimate is
gone: "The lights have gone out in the sky. Blow on the
coal of the heart."

While the fade-out of transactions with the divine begins and moves apace without conscious design in most
persons, once the contours of godlessness become explicit, justifications and rationalizations set in with inordinate speed. This is precisely what has happened to a
group in Rome whom Paul challenges in his epistle. With
a forthrightness and logic equal to the occasion, he lays
bare what he understands to be the truth about them and
their situation.

"For the wrath of God is revealed from heaven against
all ungodliness and wickedness of men. . . . Although
they knew God they did not honor him as God . . . but
became futile in their thinking and their senseless minds
were darkened. . . . Therefore God gave them up in the
lusts of their hearts to impurity, . . . to dishonorable pas-

sions, . . . to a base mind and to improper conduct. . . .
Full of envy, murder, strife, deceit, malignity, they are
gossips, slanderers, haters of God, . . . inventors of evil."
(Rom. 1:18-30.)

Although Paul is addressing himself to those in Rome
who rather virtuously identify themselves as godless, he
is also taking on those of us for whom the God relationship is faint or infrequent. And he sets against us the
claim that the problem isn't what we think it is. Many of
us defend the sparsity of our dealings with the divine on
the grounds that the evidence for his existence is wanting.
With considerable impatience Paul challenges those who
take that stance: "What can be known about God is plain
to them, because God has shown it to them. Ever since
the creation of the world his invisible nature, namely, his
eternal power and deity, has been clearly perceived in the
things that have been made. So they are without excuse;
for although they knew God they did not honor him as
God" (Rom. 1:19-21). Now Paul is not mounting an
argument for the existence of God or asserting that man
knows God instinctively. What he is saying is that the
raw materials for that knowledge are available. The problem is not a dearth of evidence but an unwillingness to
deal with it. We have chosen to exchange "the truth about
God for a lie and . . . [worship] and . . . [serve] the creature rather than the Creator" (Rom. 1:25).

Thus the charge against us is that we don't want the
God we could know, that we vaccinate ourselves against
divinity because we don't want to live with the demands
he would make upon us. The radical theologians of our
day look to Friedrich Nietzsche in defense of their claim
that "God is dead." But I suspect they fail to understand
that Nietzsche was accusing man of deicide. Listen to
these words from *Thus Spake Zarathustra:* "He *had to*

die: he looked with eyes which beheld everything,—he beheld man's . . . hidden ignominy and ugliness. His pity knew no modesty; he crept into my dirtest corners. This most prying, over-intrusive, over-pitiful one had to die. He ever beheld me: on such a witness I would have revenge—or not live myself. . . . Man cannot endure that such a witness should live."[17] Nietzsche's point is that we deny what we cannot endure. To affirm it would be an impingement on our privacy and a threat to our autonomy.

In earlier chapters I have been arguing that the difficulty many of us have in speaking and relating to God is a breakdown of Christianity's symbol system. The traditional imagery of faith no longer makes contact with our experience; it does not link up with or define those things with which we are familiar. While we may still have a nostalgic reverence for words like "God," we would be hard put to explain to what they refer. I am still convinced that our problem involves an inability to live the symbols of faith and that if Christianity is to survive, it will have to undergo a resymbolization. But what Paul has been saying broadens the issue: what is involved is our receptivity to that about which the symbols speak. Symbols require recipients who are bold enough to be affected by what they see and hear. The problem for many of us is that we have not wanted to acknowledge the symbols for the demands that acknowledgment would make upon us.

If we were to say yes to the "shockingly indiscriminate" love of God laid bare in the person of Jesus, we would have to say no to our inclination to reject those who do not please us; if we were to say yes to the message of forgiveness that breaks loose from the cross, we would have to say no to the impulse to hurt those who have hurt us; if we were to say yes to the claim that God has given us life and holds us responsible for the way we spend it, we would have to say no to the trivia and waste in which we are engaged; if we were to say yes to the message that our neighbor is the one through whom we express our love or hate toward God, we would have to say no to the pettiness, indifference, and hostility that come so naturally. And in saying no we deny what we cannot endure. I wonder if this is not why Kierkegaard said that "the nearer to God, the more pain." That has always offended me because I have assumed that to be in the presence of God would be a very joyful and pleasing experience. But it isn't, not at first. It's discomforting and distressing, some say terrifying. The person who is gazed upon from beyond has to admit things about himself he would rather ignore, he has to assume responsibilities to which he would rather be indifferent, and he has to live with claims upon the depths of his being he would rather avoid. There's pain in the presence of God, never let anyone tell you otherwise.

That may offend you, even repulse you, but let me remind you that there is always pain in love. If you have ever really loved someone, you know that. Allowing someone to bare the truth about you is a source of distress as well as joy; being responsible for the well-being of another is a burden as well as a privilege; meeting the demands of love in every moment is as strenuous as it is exhilarating. It hurts to love someone, because that level of commitment to another sets boundaries to one's love of self. D. H. Lawrence once said that it is an awful thing to fall out of the hands of God, but it might also be said that it is an awful thing to fall into them—unless, of course, you prefer the pain of reality to the saccharine of illusion.

We all have our own ways of denying what we cannot endure without putting it that starkly. Some people say they're not sure there is a God; they'll wait for more evidence, if it's forthcoming. Others say that faith is not intellectually respectable and proceed to trust other things as if that were not faith. Then others of us try to distort this God into something upon which we have claims and make of him an errand boy. But Paul cuts through this morass of rationalizations with the word that God is determined to live with us as the kind of God he is, showing no respect for our evasions and illusions. He is making himself known to you in every moment and movement of your being—in the wonders of his creation, in the very mystery of your being, in your interaction with one another, and, most forcefully, in that strange figure of the first century whom some call "Christ." "Ever since the creation of the world his invisible nature, namely, his eternal power and deity, has been clearly perceived in the things that have been made." (Rom. 1:20.) All that is required of you is to confess from the depth of your being that there is a God who works like that and then get involved in what he's doing to make human life more human. That means beginning to love others in the indiscriminate way you are loved, forgiving others in the absurd manner you have been forgiven when you least deserved it, and taking on the burdens of your neighbor in the manner yours have been assumed by him. That kind of faith takes your life away, but it gives it back with the power to stand upright in even the darkest moment of time.

For free men and women there are only two options: Either *deny* what you cannot endure or *endure* what you cannot deny. The choice is yours.

6

"Who's Afraid of Virginia Woolf?"

It is two A.M. The setting is a living room on the campus of a New England college. George, forty-six, a graying associate professor of history, and Martha, fifty-two, the boisterous daughter of the college president, are returning home from a faculty party. From the moment the front door is recklessly flung open, we witness a man and woman tear at each other without mercy. When Martha announces that she has invited guests for a post-party party, we assume the strife will be repressed. That illusion is quickly exploded as George appears to delight in opening the front door to their guests just as Martha intones a foul epithet. Nick is a tweedy and ambitious new appointee to the biology department; Honey is his birdlike wife who all evening alternates upchucking with sipping brandy. While they have come to further Nick's career by attentiveness to the president's daughter, neither is prepared for the devious encounter that is to follow. The author, Edward Albee, entitles the sequence of events "Fun and Games." But it soon becomes apparent that the game is exposing one another and the fun is only recognizable to a sadist.

The first game is "Humiliate the Host" and Martha leads off. "George," she announces, "is bogged down in the History Department." With disdain in her voice she says, "He's an old bog in the History Department, that's what George is."[18] Twenty years earlier she had imagined he would become chairman and with her father had conceived of him as president. But he failed to measure up.

> MARTHA: . . . You see, George didn't have much
> ... push ... he wasn't particularly ...
> aggressive. In fact he was sort of a ...
> . . . FLOP! A great ... big ... fat ...
> FLOP!
>
> . . .
>
> . . . [and] he can't make anything out
> of himself, somebody without the *guts* to
> make anybody proud of him . . .[19]

In time she cuts deeper into his dignity. George has written a novel about a boy who at fifteen accidentally killed his mother with a shotgun and the following summer was at the wheel in a collision in which his father was killed. Martha proceeds to announce that it wasn't really a novel, nor was the death an accident; it was the story of George's childhood. Turning toward her husband, she sneeringly shouts, "Murderer." That is "Humiliate the Host."

Now it is George's turn to introduce a game and this time it is "Get the Guests." It's played in the form of a story with George as narrator.

> GEORGE: Well, it's an allegory, really . . . . ..
> and it's all about a nice young couple.
> . . . He's blond and about thirty, . . .
> a scientist ... and his mouse is a wifey
> little type who gargles brandy all the
> time ... . ..
>
> . . .
>
> . . . And Mousie's father was a holy
> man, see, and he ran sort of a traveling

> clip joint, based on Christ . . . , and
> he took the faithful . . .[20]

Eventually he died and left the money he had conned
from the devout to Mousie. When Blondie and Mousie
were married, people wondered what he saw in her. She
was simple, sickly, and sexless. But she had money and
Blondie wanted that. "Oh," George interrupts, "we get a
flashback here, to 'How They Got Married.' "[21] This in-
troduces a game within a game.

> GEORGE: . . . The Mouse got all puffed up one
> day, and she went over to Blondie's
> house, and she stuck out her puff, and
> she said . . . look at me.
>
> . . .
>
> . . . and so they were married. . . .
>
> . . .
>
> . . . and then the puff went *away* . . . like
> magic . . . pouf![22]

That's how you play "Get the Guests," for Nick is the
opportunist who is solicitous of Honey because of her
wealth and Honey is the mouse who trapped Blondie with
a hysterical pregnancy.

There is a third game and Martha bears the brunt of it.
It's called "Bringing Up Baby." The baby is a nonexistent
son who has become a sheer emotional necessity for
Martha in particular. The illusion that he does exist indi-
cates the aridity of their marriage. For Martha, this fantasy has become so real that she can recall the birth pain,
his fine black hair when she first saw him, how at three
he broke an arm fleeing from a cow, and how she coddled
and cajoled him into becoming a man despite having a
flop for a father. She has even planned to celebrate his
twenty-first birthday on the next day. When she speaks of
him, her life seems full and focused; she has meaning in

her life and a reason to live. Against this background
George begins the game.

> GEORGE: . . . Some rather sad news.
>
> . . . While you were out of the room,
> . . . the doorbell rang. . . .
>
> . . . It was good old Western Union.
>
> . . . And he had a telegram, and it was
> for us. . . .
>
> . . . Well, Martha . . . I'm afraid our
> boy isn't coming home for his birthday.
>
> He was . . . killed . . . late in the after-
> noon. . . . . . . on a country road
> . . .
>
> . . . large tree.
>
> . . . Our son is DEAD! Can you get that
> into your head?
>
> . . . He's dead. POUF! Just like that!
> Now, how do you like it?[3]

With that game, Martha is exposed.

There's the play in outline. It's a series of games in
which George and Martha peel off layer after layer until
all illusions are destroyed, every devious motivation is
identified, and all their protective rationalizations are dis-
solved. When I saw the play on Broadway, my first reaction was this: Albee is simply portraying an utterly
nauseous and corrosive relationship and in the process revealing his own vile appraisal of human nature. It seemed
to me then that Martha and George had no other inten-

tion than to destroy each other and to drag Nick and
Honey down with them. But with further reflection I have
come to believe that there is a positive, even redeeming,
theme running through the play. It centers on the struggle
of two persons to begin living nearer to the truth about
themselves, to divest themselves of the fantasies and illusions that have destroyed their relationship, to be present
to each other and themselves as the persons they really
are. Edward Albee provides the clue when he entitles the
third act "The Exorcism."

Here it becomes clear that they are not out to destroy
each other but to destroy everything that prevents their
living an honest and meaningful life. The death of the
nonexistent son is a culmination of what has been happening throughout the play. They challenge each other to
live without illusion, to face up to their lives without false
props, to function with a minimum of fantasy. They want
more than anything to be free of the little games by which
they have avoided life as it really is. They want to truly
live and to live truly. Both the terror and the necessity of
that are focused in the last exchange between them. Nick
and Honey have left and the older couple are alone. After
a long silence Martha speaks, alluding to the exorcism of
the nonexistent son.

MARTHA: . . . Did you . . . did you . . . have to?
GEORGE: (*Pause*) Yes.

. . .

MARTHA: I don't know.
GEORGE: It was . . . time.
MARTHA: Was it?
GEORGE: Yes.

. . .

(*Long silence*) It will be better.
MARTHA: (*Long silence*) I don't . . . know.

GEORGE: It will be ... maybe.
MARTHA: I'm ... not ... sure.

. . .

       Just ... us?
GEORGE: Yes.
MARTHA: I don't suppose, maybe, we could. ...
GEORGE: No. Martha.

. . .

       Are you all right?
MARTHA: Yes. No.
GEORGE: (*Puts his hand gently on her shoulder;
       she puts her head back and he sings to
       her, very softly*)
       Who's afraid of Virginia Woolf
                Virginia Woolf
                Virginia Woolf,
     [Who's afraid to live without illusion?]
MARTHA: I ... am ... George. ...[24]

George nods, slowly, sensing his own pain as well as hers, yet aware that only the pain of truth can free them for each other, only by dying to all that is false and phony can they be reconciled to life. And as the curtain is drawn, one has the feeling that this is not the end of life but the beginning of it.

Now I make bold to suggest that whether Mr. Albee is aware of it or not, he has dramatized a theme central to the Christian faith. It is the experience of being freed by truth. In the Fourth Gospel, Jesus is reported to have said: "You will know the truth, and the truth will make you free" (John 8:32). At another point he says, "I am ... the truth" (John 14:6). Stark and startling as it may sound, I contend that what has happened between George and Martha is a repetition of the Christ event. The word "Christ," of course, refers to an event in history identified with a particular person at a particular time and a particular place. But it also refers to the possibility that what happened once can happen again. What the early Christians experienced in the person of Christ, and later when he was no longer there in person, was the truth about themselves in a way that set them free. What he gave them was the realization they could live again.

The writer of John focuses this with the story of a woman brought before Jesus by the scribes and the Pharisees who have caught her in the act of adultery (John 8:3-11). They ask Jesus what should be done with her, knowing that the law of Moses prescribed death by stoning. Pretending at first to ignore the trap they have set for him, he suddenly turns on them and says, "Let him who is without sin among you be the first to throw a stone at her." The scribes and Pharisees stand revealed, and disappear leaving Jesus with the woman. He looks up at her and says: "Woman, where are . . . [your accusers]? Has no one condemned you?" She replies, "No one, Lord." And then he said to her, "Neither do I condemn you: go, and do not sin again." In effect he says, "I know what you are, but you need not be what you have been." By that confrontation with truth, she is set free to live again. This is what the New Testament writers mean by Christ: Being set free by the truth.

We are all afraid of Virginia Woolf. Like Martha, we are afraid to live our lives without illusions, rationalizations, and false props. But there is one who comes to each of us and says, "I know what you are, but you need not be what you have been." The words may be spoken by a friend, a lover, a parent, even a casual acquaintance. But they are only the mediators of grace. The message comes to us from one who is the Truth about life and by whose Truth we are free to live.

7

The Perimeter of Christianity

One of the central issues for a number of people in our time is whether or not they can in good conscience identify themselves as Christians. Their hesitancy is rather refreshing. Too many for too long have glibly assumed the label without any awareness of what it means or the demands it puts upon a person. While some are anxious to be counted in "just in case Christianity turns out to be true," the majority are cautious because they do not want to presume upon a noble tradition in which they have participated fragmentarily. A young woman of substantial integrity, who was driven by a passionate desire to secure herself to a meaning for her life, framed the question thus: "Is it possible to be participating in the substance of faith without sharing its rituals or accepting its symbols?"

That defines the issue rather neatly and almost demands a negative response. Whether or not one is a theologian, one must respect the intrinsic relationship between form and content. Man is a symbolizing and ritualizing creature who builds meanings into images and acts that cannot easily be transposed. If you doubt that, let a young man offer to the lady of his choice a bracelet instead of a ring and see if she can accept it as a symbol of their engagement. In our culture being engaged and wearing an engagement ring are bound together. Thus one is tempted to argue that the Christian meanings and the traditional ways in which they are expressed and celebrated belong together. Yet every human contention, even those we declare most absolutely, has its qualifications. And this affirmation of the integrity of form and content is relativized by that "freedom of God" which Karl Barth forever sets before our thinking. The God of the Biblical faith is certainly not limited to those forms through which we have traditionally acknowledged and remembered his presence. Perhaps we need now to learn the hard lesson of the Jews in the first century: God isn't even totally committed to the chosen people, he can bypass them when it serves his purposes. This "freedom of God" demands that we be prepared for him to invade our lives in ways and forms and through persons that he never has before. Perhaps there are times when we give him no other choice!

It may be helpful to wrestle with our concern by talking about the perimeter of Christianity. The geometric image not only designates the outer boundary of a body but that which stands less self-consciously under the influence of the center. It suggests that those on the fringe may be participating in the substance of faith without being fully aware of it.

I

The most important thing on the perimeter of Christianity is not the affirmations that are made but the questions that are raised. The mistake most of us make in assessing our relationship to Christianity is that we measure ourselves against its conclusions. We stand up against the claims that Christ is divine, that the Bible is inspired, and that God controls history and we become disillusioned by our inability to appropriate them. Then we resemble Alice in Wonderland, who told the Queen of Hearts that she attempted to believe ten impossible things each day before breakfast. With that approach shot, we have no chance of landing on the green. We must begin with the questions it raises before we can resonate with its affirmations. Some years ago when George Buttrick was University Preacher at Harvard, he invited Archibald MacLeish to lead in worship. The poet refused, rather abruptly. Later in the afternoon MacLeish phoned to apologize for his manner but also to explain that he could not accept the assignment in good conscience. Buttrick understood and thought no more of it. But that evening the phone rang in his home, and it was the poet again. "Hello, George, this is Archie. I'll do it. But one thing must be clear. I'm not convinced that Christianity has the answers we are looking for—but I do think it has the right questions."[25] As far as I am concerned, that's all it takes to be on the perimeter of Christianity. The issue is not one's ability to accept the answers but to identify with the questions.

To develop that point, I want to wrestle with one of them: What can I trust? Where can I invest myself and not be cheated? I submit that this is one of the most significant questions any of us asks. Like Captain Ahab in Melville's *Moby Dick,* we need "to feel something in this slippery world that can hold."[26] Call that a crutch if you must. It may be that. But I have never seen a man without one. We all stand in need of something to which we can give infinite attention, something that can elicit from us unconditional devotion, and something we can cling to with ultimate passion.

Yet we seldom ask the question of trust in its pure form. It comes wrapped up in an intense experience. For many it is mounted in the mood of disillusionment, when things we trusted gave out. A set of parents may have felt safe in the expectation that their son would have four years in college and perhaps a few beyond that free of the draft. But then the war in Vietnam boiled over, and they realized that they could not count on what had seemed so sure. Young persons may have invested themselves generously in a love relationship with the expectation that they might spend their lives together. Then what was between them gave out leaving one or both wondering if they could risk involvement again. Or any of us can be unnerved by the ever-present absurdities of life. Our trust in life's goodness can be destroyed when death upends its harmony; the betrayal of us by a person whose loyalty we never questioned can lead to cynicism about friendship; a freak twist of events can reverse a promising career and leave as its mark bitterness and resentment.

But the question of trust can be just as real when we feel on top of the world, when we have the feeling that life is too good to be true. We don't have to be down in the dumps to ask it. As we look to the future, we may wonder how we can maintain all we have going for us. The joy of life is a frail thing. How can we guarantee that the close friendships we have in one place will be ours when we move to another, that we will continue to find our responsibilities in our job or home meaningful and fulfilling, that we will be able to succeed in future tasks as we have in past ones?

In yet another person the question of trust may be present in the form of a denial that anything can be trusted. In him the concern is expressed in a passionate rage against anything that presents itself as trustworthy. There's at least a fragment of that in all of us. But implicit in the negation is usually a search for something to rely upon. I believe, for example, that those who rail most vigorously against the Christian faith take it more seriously than many who embrace it. This must have been what led Luther to write that "nobody in this life is nearer to God than those who hate and deny him, and he has no more pleasing, no more dear children than these."[27] Consent always lies at the heart of dissent. It's an inverted form of faith.

Up to this point all I am asking of those on the perimeter of Christianity is that they identify themselves with the question of trust.

II

But now I want to move from the center and press its claim of faith toward the perimeter. It is affirmed in The Second Letter of Paul to the Corinthians. "If any one is in Christ, he is a new creation; the old has passed away, behold, the new has come." (II Cor. 5:17.) Paul's contention is that Christ points him toward what can be trusted. This Jesus of Nazareth holds him up against something that is ultimately Real and really Ultimate. This figure of flesh and blood confronts him with what "in this slippery world" a man can hold on to and not be deceived. You may not like his certainty or his exclusiveness, but it comes at us with the contention that if you trust fully anything less, you are backing the wrong horse. The British historian Herbert Butterfield sets the claim in unconditional terms: "Hold to Christ, and for the rest be totally uncommitted."[28]

That is the claim faith sets upon us. But what does Paul mean when he says, "If any one is *in Christ?*" Some might say it's a matter of being enraptured with a figure both human and divine. Others might claim it is a matter of being fascinated with a person who represents man at his best. Still others might say it is a matter of struggling to fulfill his teachings. Each may be part of the process. But they are not the heart of what it means to be "in Christ" and never were. The unknown visionary who wrote the book of Revelation identifies it in terms of experiencing life as being made new. He puts it in a rather archaic way but listen anyway: "Then I saw a new heaven and a new earth; for the first heaven and the first earth had passed away. . . . And I heard a great voice from the throne saying, 'Behold, the dwelling of God is with men. . . . The former things have passed away. . . . *I make all things new*' " (Rev. 21:1-5). Cut through the imagery of antiquity and you have what it means to be in Christ. It is to experience in the midst of all that is old, stale, and decadent its transformation into something new. This is why Paul Tillich calls Jesus "the New Being." He stands for the possibility that every moment of life can be made over into what it ought to be. The Christian faith bids us trust that our life can be made new.

But many of us want to protest that we have not participated in anything like that. At times the old has such a stranglehold upon our lives that the promise of something new is vacuous if not offensive. I cannot argue with that feeling; it's as real as life itself. But have there not been moments in which life's hostile facade has been accosted and overcome, when the old has been broken down and you have been in the presence of newness? It may have been a moment in which the meaninglessness of your life gave way under the pressure of a task you felt destined to fulfill. It may have been a moment in which the coldness and indifference of those about you were transformed into warmth and concern. It may have been a moment in which your anxiety about life was overcome by the courage to engage it without fear. It may have been a moment in which you recognized the humanness of one who had been an object of hate or scorn. Or it may have been a moment in which you looked into the eyes of another and responded to his need. You can chalk it all up to chance if you like. But the Christian faith understands these moments as ones in which God is present making all things new.

Now let me return to the question with which I began: Is it possible to be participating in the substance of the Christian faith without sharing its rituals or accepting its symbols? And the answer is yes. You are on the perimeter of Christianity if you can identify with its questions; you are moving in toward its center if you have experienced moments in which all things are made new. All I can do now is to invite you to explore the possibility that you are "in Christ," and that the forms of faith may be the fullest way to celebrate that identity.

8

Christianity Without Religion

If you have been to the film *La Dolce Vita,* you may remember the first scene. A magnificent statue of Christ, suspended incongruously from a helicopter, is being transported across Rome. It passes over decaying arches that two thousand years ago channeled water into the city, provoking comparison for glory lost. The shadow of Christ sweeps across a soccer field reminding one of the ghostly and phantom effect of religion. Finally, it hovers over a rooftop where bikini-attired women inhale the sun. With subtle indifference one asks, "What is it?" Another replies: "It's Christ. But where is he going?" A third responds, "To the Pope."[29] Then they turn their attention to the pilot, who propositions them for bed.

Author and director Frederico Fellini seems to be saying that religion—the embodiment of belief in creed, institution, and ritual—no longer makes a claim upon us. The forms of faith are lifeless, impotent, and without meaning. What in another time sparked devotion now evokes indifference at best and at worst passes by unnoticed. To paraphrase Nietzsche, religion is dead, the heart no longer beats within it, it is the tomb of God.

Jesus came up against this phenomenon in the Pharisees. While purporting to keep the faith alive, they destroyed it with sterilized practices, routine rituals, and facile confessions. One day they came to Jesus with the report that his disciples had desecrated the Sabbath by plucking grain to still their hunger. Believing that faith was sustained by laws and tradition, they demanded strict adherence. To them Jesus said, "I tell you, something greater than the temple is here" (Matt. 12:6). There is more to the faith than the forms in which it is expressed.

While in the previous chapter we examined the possibility of experiencing the substance of faith without participating in the forms, now we are to explore the means of aligning ourselves more fully with that substance. How can we find that something greater than the temple? How can we have Christianity without religion?

I

We can begin with the determination to live in the world without God. This is not an experiment calculated to prove its own futility; neither is it a denial of the Transcendent. That we assume radical responsibility for our own existence is a demand the Christian faith makes upon us. The implications of this are extreme, and many persons will be distressed. No one likes his security threatened, even when he suspects that it is false. But faith begins with the realization that we are forsaken, cast into the world without benefit of a divine helpmate. The authority for that is none other than the New Testament. From the cross Jesus raises the human question, "My God, my God, why hast thou forsaken me?" (Matt. 27:46). Silence is the answer, a silence which casts man back upon himself. Jesus understood what the silence meant, for moments later he said, "Into thy hands I commit my spirit!" (Luke 23:46). God is to be trusted with our destiny, not used in our present.

Few have grasped the depth of this more surely than Dietrich Bonhoeffer, a German theologian imprisoned by the Nazis. Before they hanged him he wrote the guidelines for a new theology. The relevant one is this: "Honesty demands that we live in the world as if there were no God. . . . God himself . . . makes us know that we must live as men who can get along without him. The God who is with us is the God who forsakes us. . . . We stand continually in the presence of the God who makes us live in the world without the God-hypothesis."[30]

The true act of faith is the willingness to stand naked and alone, resolutely responsible for one's own existence, without resort to the God hypothesis as an escape from reality. And the honesty demanded of Christians is the determination to face existence without illusionary hopes, to stand in wonder and tears before the unexplainable without importing a theistic rationale, to pursue causes we see as worthy without claiming divine sanction, to step forward into each day as men who suffer and die without the fantasy that God saves his own from misery. That may sound like humanism and stoicism; it has affinities to both. But it is the stance of one resolved to trust God without using him, to live before God without employing the God hypothesis against him.

When Jesus said, "Something greater than the temple is here," he was castigating religion, the contraptions men employ to secure the services of God. This is why Karl Barth calls religion unbelief, the affair of godless men.[31] It is their trust in pietistic practices to maneuver the divine. Only when this temple is destroyed, when the luxury of the God hypothesis is denied, is faith a possibility. We are called by God to live in the world without him.

II

With this in mind, we can make bold to forget for now the doctrines and creeds, the subtle and sophisticated symbols, the institutions and rituals which mean nothing to us. No one ever came into faith through the repetition of meaningless confessions and pietistic practices. The genesis of faith is not the fact that men have to believe but that they have to live. What has become known as the Christian faith was a question about life before it was an affirmation about God. The author of Genesis could not write, "In the beginning God created the heavens and the earth" (Gen. 1:1), until he had pondered why there was life. The psalmist could not sing, "The LORD is my shepherd" (Ps. 23:1), until he had struggled with aimlessness and futility. Job could not claim, "I know that my Redeemer lives" (Job 19:25), until he had agonized with the misery of his existence. Paul could not affirm, "We know that in everything God works for good" (Rom. 8:28), until he had been pestered by that "thorn . . . in the flesh" (II Cor. 12:7). Faith comes only to those who face the questions raised by being alive and self-conscious.

Thus, the task of faithful man is to wrestle affectionately with the pressure points in his life. What does it mean that I will one day die, that my life has a boundary I cannot remove? Why do I do the things I do—hate when I profess to love, seek revenge when I know the honor of forgiveness, take the wrong course when I know the right? What is the reality to which I refer with the word "me"— am I the brutal impulses I find within myself or am I made of nobler stuff? Why am I here at this particular time and place in the world—is there a destiny to be fulfilled or tragic circumstances to be endured? Can I be free of the guilt that binds me, the despair that curses me, the loneli-

ness that separates me from others? Why does the world
appear against me—take from me those I love and need,
put me at the mercy of men without honor, frustrate my
ambitions and aspirations?

These concerns are the womb of faith, the birthplace of
confession. In matters of belief, man is born not with a
creed but with a question. To ask forever the innocent and
searching questions of a child is his task. This in part is
what Jesus meant when he said, "Unless you turn and become like children, you will never enter the kingdom of
heaven" (Matt. 18:3). The glory and worth of man is that
he can raise the questions of existence and stand resolute
before them. The joy of the Christian life is that by grace
these questions become the portals of faith. That something greater than the temple is brought into the vision of
the man who stares into the abyss of his own existence
until he sees beyond it.

III

We have suggested two approaches to the Christian
faith when religion has become meaningless, when the
temple is an obstruction. Now we must turn to content:
that something greater than the temple is Christ himself.
He is the one through whom we can come to trust God
without using the God hypothesis; he is the one toward
whom the questions of existence point.

But here it is difficult to speak with meaning and precision. For us Christ is a "fading image" blurred by use and
misuse. While his name is held in honor, his life recalled
for inspiration, his words read and preached upon, "his
figure has been rubbed flat by custom and routine; he
neither shocks nor surprises. . . . His mystery has eva-
orated, his power vanished, his thrust broken. W

finally absorbed him, made him our own, and dare re-shape his countenance to fit our depraved and vulgar tastes."[32] We can reflect upon the titles and allusions to him in the New Testament, but few if any put us in touch with the reality of his person. What can it mean to us that others have called him Lord, Messiah, the Son of God, the Word made flesh?

In each day men must struggle with him until a new image is born, one that pumps blood into his lifeless form. Let me suggest an image, not adequate or original, but meaningful to me. It's Christ the clown! That may shock and offend, but toy with the image a moment. In the joyfulness of his antics and the sorrow of his face, the clown embraces the full dimensions of existence In spoofing our pretensions, he frees us of their power. He appears weak and harmless, yet moves men in directions an army could not force. Foolishness and folly are his stock-in-trade, yet they are rooted in love and in wisdom. While victim of our ridicule and disdain, he is victor in forgiving what we have done. He degrades himself before us, stooping to all that is distorted within us, yet restores us to what we were meant to be. He is tender but not sentimental, compassionate but not soft, selfless but not anemic, and works on us until we imitate his way. He gives himself that we may find ourselves. The image of Christ the clown cannot bear the weight of his person, no image can. But wrestle with it until something of his reality comes into view. Then you will have been grasped by that something greater than the temple, the one in whom we can have Christianity without religion.

9

The Purposes of God

One of the substantive claims of faith that many of us find both intriguing and exasperating is identified with the word "providence," the belief that God has something to do with all the events of life. There's a side of me which knows better than to believe that, which wants to see it as a bit of pious optimism nourished in faith's ivory tower. It calls to mind a conversation with a friend whose financial situation was critical. Unexpectedly she was left some money by a distant relative. With a sigh of relief, she exclaimed, "The good Lord took care of me!" It was all I could do to keep from saying: "Oh, no, your great-aunt died and willed you an inheritance. There's a natural sequence of events which explains it." I can't believe in a celestial manipulator who prearranges and rearranges life to suit our fancy. We might wish it were so, and at times we convince ourselves it is. There's comfort in the belief that God holds every force and factor in tow, stands forever ready to organize existence to our benefit. It takes all the worry and the effort out of life, and, I might add, all the responsibility and creativity as well. If that's the way faith would have it, I'll cast my lot with secular man and his assertion that things happen because they happen. At best it's an illusion to claim that God structures all the moments of life.

I've got to deny that, and in defense of God! If I give him full credit for all the good things in life, I'd have to give him blame for all the bad. I could not forgive him for taking my father from me when I was but eleven, for making my wife's brother a spastic who cannot speak or hear or control his body in normal ways, for causing the accidents that led to the deaths of two students last summer, and for creating a world in which men suffer and die on battlefields. We can't have it just one way—it's shoddy accounting to record the credits and not the debits. If we want to perceive him as a celestial manipulator, then on one day we may sing, "Praise God from whom all blessings flow," but on another, "Curse him from whom evil flows, as well." Let's be honest about that.

Now there is another side of me that wants to see things through "the eyes of faith." And here the record is clear. Every page of Scripture is drenched with the claim that God has much to do with what happens. Genesis tells us that God's Spirit brooded over the abyss and caused the world to be. Moses believed that God led the Israelites out of bondage in Egypt and formed them into a holy people. The Wisdom writers saw him as the one who clothes the lilies of the field, feeds the ravens, numbers the very hairs of our heads, sends the rain upon the just and the unjust alike. The psalmist extols the God who holds the whole creation in the palm of his hand. Paul claimed of all things that his thorn in the flesh had been given to him with a purpose. And Jesus accepted the events of his life, even the cross, as willed by his Father. The Bible will not be free of the notion that God is Lord of life. And I am less free to be so cavalier when confronted by it

So with one mind to rule God out and another to read

him in, let's examine a classic formulation of providence: "We know," writes Paul, "that in everything God works for good with those who love him, who are called according to his purpose" (Rom. 8:28).

I

Now I am struck by what is *not* said in that sentence. Nothing suggests that there is a celestial manipulator prearranging and rearranging life, causing one car to stop in time to save a child's life and another after it's too late. There's no suggestion that our lives are engineered from on high. The normal structures of events are recognized and preserved, the network of predictable cause and effect remains intact. God doesn't sit at a gigantic switchboard calling all the signals. And that says something about where at times our trust and responsibility belong. Several years ago I flew in a new jet airplane, a model that at the time had been accident-prone. My first inclination when the plane began to shake and the pilot called for seat belts was to cover the occasion with a quick prayer. Remembering pictures of jets that had crashed, I was prepared to try anything from "Hail Marys" to giving up James Bond movies if allowed to live! But then it occurred to me what I was making of God—a tyrant who rearranges, interrupts, or otherwise takes over from the laws of nature and machines. That's superstition born of wishful thinking. Even if God would accept that role, I wouldn't want it at other times. It would reduce me to something less than a person with freedom and responsibility. At this point I decided to trust the pilot and resign myself to what might happen. That may sound faithless and pagan, but there is nothing in Paul's statement that suggests it. He does not claim that God overrules natural occurrences and inevitable events.

What he does say is that God is at work "in everything," that at every moment he is purposefully present. In every event he is working through the normal structures of life and the freedom we have within them willing our ultimate fulfillment, creating new possibilities for us, never allowing the final word to be futility and defeat. Another Paul, Paul Tillich, says it in a way meaningful to me: "Providence means that there is a creative and saving possibility implied in every situation, . . . that the demonic and destructive forces within ourselves and our world can never have an unbreakable grasp upon us, and that the bond which connects us with his fulfilling love can never be destroyed."[33] God has to do with what may come of what happens to us, forever guaranteeing that it will reflect his loving purpose. God didn't take my father from me at eleven: heart failure caused his death; he didn't cause my wife's brother to be a spastic: there was a mishap at birth; he didn't determine the deaths of two students last summer: a failure of judgment was involved; he didn't decree that men should suffer and die on battlefields: malice and greed are the cause. But in each event there were and there remain creative and saving possibilities. God is purposefully present, luring and driving us toward them through finite conditions. This means to faith that ultimately nothing in life is tragic, the resources of grace may be resisted but they are not withdrawn. The cross is symbol and guarantee of that. There's the testimony that while God doesn't will all the things that happen to us, he wills something through them.

II

But Paul would not have us understand this only as a promise; it is a responsibility as well. He says that God is at work "in everything" among men who are "called according to his purpose." That's where the claim rests upon us, and not lightly either! In a previous chapter we quoted a fragment of a letter Dietrich Bonhoeffer had written from prison. Those same words speak again to the issue before us now. "I'm sure everything that happens to me has a purpose, even though it cuts right across my own wishes. As I see it, I am here in prison for a purpose, and I only hope that I am living up to it."[34] That's what faith in providence does to a man: it causes him to search himself to see if he is living up to it.

Of course, this leaves us with a question difficult to answer: How shall we recognize those threads of purpose weaving their way through causal networks and natural occurrences; how can we detect the will of God? That is a question we will have forever to ask and never fully answer. His way with creation eludes human definition and measurement. You see the danger, don't you? Our eager and egocentric little lives are all too ready to take some petty purpose of our own and bless it with God's name. I caught a taste of that in an analysis of the economy by a stockbroker at the beginning of the year. Looking over the year—the growth of the gross national product, industries' commitment to capital improvement, dividends at new highs, the stock market pacing itself nicely—he then exclaimed, "Thank God, he's on our side!" That equation of God with our successes and desires is illusion at best and treason at worst.

Yet while we cannot pin down the purposes of God or name the particulars as we might like, we can catch glimpses of them. For the threads of purpose now look strangely like what we have seen before—deeds and words conceived to make human life more human, events shaped to grant healing and wholeness to man. We have a model for that in the Man who lived for others, whose life took the shape of concern and care for all that warps and distorts us. The purposes of God look like his word of acceptance to the despised tax collector, his word of forgiveness to the woman who sold her body, the word of hope to the bereaved without it. The purposes of God look like his act of feeding those whose bodies stood still with hunger, his act of sharing the deepest mysteries of life, his act of giving himself for others. When these things begin to happen, then the purposes of God for man are weaving their way through the laws of nature and the contingencies of life.

So providence comes upon us as a claim, as a calling to be a part of what God is doing in the world to make human life more human. Once it has touched your heart you can't be indifferent to the cries of persons in need, you can't be idle and complacent as if history would run its own course to the benefit of man, you can't sit back absorbing all the good things of life without sharing them. You have got to identify the saving and healing possibilities in each moment and allow all that you are to be instrumental in their fulfillment.

We may question the providence of God; perhaps we must. But it questions us as well: What are we doing amid the purposes of God?

10

The Hell of Hell

One does not have to be on the perimeter of Christianity to be disturbed by references to hell. Both skeptic and solid citizens of faith maintain a rather quaint picture of what it is like: It focuses on a cosmic bonfire beneath the earth attended by red devils with pitchforks roasting the damned. While Dante, Milton, and Michelangelo have done much to foster this vision, the New Testament is not without blame. In the Sermon on the Mount, Jesus is represented as saying that whoever calls another a fool "shall be liable to the hell of fire" (Matt. 5:22). And the author of Revelation cannot resist a reference to the destiny of the wicked: They will be "tormented with fire and brimstone" (Rev. 14:10).

Yet for all the implications that hell is a "specific region" on a "cosmic map," it can be interpreted as a symbol for a state of existence. This is apparent if we examine several contexts in which the word is used. When David is in anguish because of his betrayal at the hands of Saul, he expresses it by saying, "The cords of hell entangled me" (II Sam. 22:6). When the psalmist is in a state of personal stress, he refers to what he is experiencing as "the snares of hell" (Ps. 116:3). And when Jonah is agonizing with his fate, it is said that he cried out to God from "the belly of hell" (Jonah 2:2).

While the vividness of the Biblical tradition implies that hell is a place, it needs to be understood as meaning an ever-present possibility in life. Inevitably it gets spatialized and temporalized, otherwise we cannot take hold of it; but the reference is to a reality in our lives now and always. To understand the depth of meaning in this symbol, it may be helpful to probe the situation of a man of whom it was said, he went to hell.

I

One sentence describes him: "There was a rich man, who was clothed in purple and fine linen and who feasted sumptuously every day" (Luke 16:19). Immediately the image comes alive of one whose self-indulgence knew no bounds. The faintest desire was sufficient justification to possess any object. In his wardrobe at one time were more garments than most men wear in a lifetime. The waste from his table would be perceived as a feast in a normal household. In him the wish to have everything was never frustrated.

But if this is all we see in him, we miss the tragedy of his situation. The self-indulgence was but a symptom of a deeper problem: He passionately loved the one thing that could not love him back; he loved himself. There was one dominant affection in his life, and he was its object. The universe came to a focus in him and in everything he sought his own. The self served as the center out of which he lived. It was the perspective from which all was viewed, the norm by which all was measured, and the focal point around which all was organized.

Now it is but a child's skip from this to a brand of existentialism with which many are intrigued. Its essential message is this: All I have in this world is myself. There are no values for me to appropriate, there is no meaning that I can embrace, there is no destiny for me to fulfill. In an indifferent and often hostile world I have to become a self against the backdrop of nothingness. My only resource is self-awareness. Even the self which is aware has no shape or content until I give it form. A glob is thrust into the universe, and I have the freedom and responsibility to fashion it into something called "me."

This has its attraction. It is rather flattering to have so much at stake with so little help from without. Who among us can resist it, at least upon first hearing? But the tragedy of the self which emerges from its own center is that it cannot bear the strain. Examine the self endlessly, and the process becomes permeated with nausea; depend upon it exclusively, and it collapses under the burden; love it solely, and that love destroys it. The self is helpless by itself. It cannot speak a word of forgiveness which will break its bondage to guilt. It cannot overcome the essential loneliness which tears at the heart. It cannot but rage against the death which is its fate. By myself I cannot even be myself.

Those of you familiar with existentialist literature know that Albert Camus was one of its chief architects. No one has with more force presented the theme that man must assert himself in an alien world and live out of his own center, for the universe is without one. But what you may not know is this: A few months before his untimely death he went and lived among a community of Huguenots, a Protestant communion with its roots in Calvinism. It is said that he had become disenchanted with the vision of a world without values, without meaning, and without purpose. What he found within himself—he had called it once "an invincible summer"—was not enough. Unless what he discovered is buried in an unpublished paper, we shall never know what happened to him in a rigorously Christian community. But perhaps it is enough for us to know that the lonely self which he had exalted and loved was insufficient. It is the one thing that cannot stand by you ultimately, the one that cannot love you back. It's hell when all you have is yourself, when the self is the center from which you attempt to live.

II

Now while it's hell enough to have one's life centered on a self which cannot withstand the strain, the anguish is infinitely deepened when that forbids engagement with another's life as well. That was the rich man's plight. "At his gate lay a poor man named Lazarus, full of sores, who desired to be fed with what fell from the rich man's table. . . . The poor man died." (Luke 16:20-22.) But the rich man did not even know that another stood in need of him.

Tennessee Williams understands this inability to relate meaningfully. Recently he wrote, "When you ignore other people completely, that is hell," when you cannot put yourself aside "to feel deeply for another person,"[35] that is the most acute form of human misery. Every play he writes is but a variation upon this theme, and some who know him say it is the dominant misery in his own life.

Who among us has not had at least a taste of that, of having people around and no meaningful relationship to them? We may have the most stylish cut of clothes, the cleanest of clean shaves, a car the cost of which would support a family for a year, but what joy is it all if we are not connected with one another? The most tragic symbol in our time is the man in a Brooks Brothers suit at the wheel of the latest sports car who is not related deeply to anyone. He has everything—and nothing. And perhaps the worst of it is that, like the rich man, we are so lost in ourselves that we do not even perceive what we are missing. He never really knew that the occasion for love was laying at his doorstep, much less that it finally died there.

In Albert Camus's *The Fall* there is a line I can never forget or ultimately escape. It hovers over my very being like a Damoclean sword. Jean-Baptiste says in a moment of terrifying insight: "I have no more friends; I have nothing but accomplices. To make up for this, their number has increased; they are the whole human race."[36] It is one thing to be lonely when by yourself, but quite another to be lonely in a crowd—to have only accomplices, no friends. Few of us are spared at least moments when there is much conversation but little communication; many persons within touch, but none within reach; a multitude of glances, but no one seeing you are there. We have known it in the home when parent and offspring are in the same room but are a world apart in understanding; we have known it in a social context where a friend entertains lavishly but does not show the care that would cost nothing; and we have felt it in the place where we work when the physical presence of many was made intolerable because of their indifference. It's the feeling that you belong deeply to no one and no one belongs deeply to you.

That's a phase of hell: The self is so centered upon itself that it cannot connect itself meaningfully with others.

III

But even this is not the ultimate hell of hell. The real misery of the rich man was that he had no relationship to anything eternal, he was exiled from the very source of life. This is the reality behind the Biblical symbol of hell. It's the place where God is not. This is the meaning of the word "Sheol," which we translate "hell." It is the state in which man is utterly separated from his Creator.

And the hell of that is finding ourselves without the possibility of renewal, of our lives ever being different than they have been. It's that eternal continuum with no break, no opportunity of a future anything but a repetition of the past. This is what tortured the rich man: Every tomorrow was but a reenactment of today. Hell was not a place to which he went or a punishment that he got; it was fixation in his present state.

Without a theistic frame of reference, this is exactly what Jean-Paul Sartre is representing in *No Exit*. Those who have thought that the point of the play was in Garcin's cry, "Hell is other people"[37] have missed the misery the author is depicting. The hell of hell is symbolized in the realization by Garcin when he arrives there that everyone's eyelids are fixed. There is no blink, no possibility of renewal that comes from the rest the eye gets from staring at the world. In hell there is no breakoff after which man can start anew. There is just the haunting stare at sameness, eyes fixed on a world that will never be different.

Though Sartre would not identify it as such, this is life outside the renewing love and grace of God, life that cannot be restored by the presence of his care. There is no freedom from what has been. A word spoken in anger is not covered over with forgiveness. A deed in violation of another corrupts forever the structure of the relationship. A failure is a failure and never a channel for new beginnings. And death is final without the promise of eternal relatedness. The hell of hell is its distance from the Ultimate Source of life and its renewing power.

It all begins with the centering of the self upon itself,

moves on to the state of no meaningful connections with one another, and reaches its climax in the absence of God himself. But Christ descended into hell; into the region of our self-enclosure, into the abortive relationships with one another, and into the very alienation from God. If anyone is in union with that Christ, he is a new being; the old state of things has passed away. The eyelids of our existence can blink again, find renewal in the love God has for us.

11

Recovering Immediacy in Prayer

It is difficult for many of us to resist purchasing the most recent book on prayer. The expectation is that the next volume we read will provide the clue we need for a meaningful experience. It seldom does. Prayer as a daily and routinized exercise is not a viable option for many in this age. The more honest would admit they don't pray as much anymore, not in the traditional sense. This is not to say that certain public prayers offered on our behalf have failed to move us, that the prayers we offer for ourselves are a hangover from childhood piety, or that we labor to maintain our intense feelings of anguish, joy, or thanksgiving on a horizontal plane. It's the routine of prayer, the nightly meditation, that has lost much of its appeal. For this dearth of piety we feel little remorse. It is beyond our grasp how saints and others through the ages have spent hours on their knees in communion with God. While we honor the rigor of their devotion, to imitate it would be dishonest.

This disenchantment with the routine of prayer is symptomatic of a deeper problem: Modern man must discover a new way with God, one that can be meaningful in an age when traditional piety has no appeal. To find him in the gaps of knowledge, between what we know and cannot understand; to perceive him as "up there" in celestial majesty; to experience him in ritual and confess him in creeds somehow escapes us, does it not? Dietrich Bonhoeffer said that we live in a "world come of age," one in which men no longer look to a transcendent realm where their longings are fulfilled. We don't need God to explain things, science can do that; we don't want God as a crutch, we can take care of ourselves; we don't see ourselves as religious, piety is not our forte. But for most of us this is being "honest to God"; it is the manner in which we take him seriously. And what we need is not a religious revival but a new understanding of what it means to be faithful and obedient.

This is the context within which the phenomenon of prayer comes under scrutiny. And the Scripture that will guide our explorations reads: "Rejoice always, pray without ceasing, in every thing give thanks" (I Thess. 5:16-18).

I

This suggests to me that prayer is not first or even primarily a routine, that time one sets aside to be with God. Yet church and home have left us with that impression. We have been taught that prayer is a time of disengagement from the world, withdrawal from the pressures of the day, in which we reflect on things divine. Who among us was not induced to end each day with, "Now I lay me down to sleep"? For years I couldn't get to sleep without it! Who among us was not induced to pause before each meal and repeat, "God is great, God is good, and I thank him for this food"? I used to think I would be struck dead if I ate without it! It is not difficult to see why we have come to think of prayer as the deference one shows the Almighty at fixed times.

But some of us will want to confess that we gave up the ritual a long time ago. When it became perfunctory and meaningless we let it go from our routine; only an occasional tinge of guilt reminds us of its absence. Perhaps the reason we gave up so easily is that we came to distrust its integrity. It has appeared to many as an evasion of responsibility, a substitute for involvement and sacrifice. We have caught ourselves relegating to God things we ought to do ourselves. And then we have sat in churches when prayers were offered for the Negro by people who would not have him for a neighbor, when prayers were offered for the poor and needy by people who would do nothing about slum conditions unless those conditions infringed upon the value of their property, when prayers were offered for love and justice by people too respectable to be engaged in causes that would fight for them. Others of us lost interest when we came to see in ourselves and others the disposition to use prayer as a shortcut to success. We are all too familiar with a generation of businessmen whom Norman Vincent Peale has taught to appeal to the God of *The Wall Street Journal* for assistance in amassing wealth. The invocation of whatever benevolent force there may be to achieve our way in the world violates our sense of honor. And then there are others who perceive it as ineffectual. Why thank God for what would have happened anyway, why confess what we have done wrong when we don't see ourselves as accountable, and why share our deepest needs and feelings when prayer is only talking to oneself? It all began in routine—but for many it has ended in rejection.

That this was the story of my own life became all too clear last summer. My little daughter Sara Jane had fallen on a sharp object which ripped open her cheek. From outside the operating room, where five stitches were being taken in her cheek, I heard: "It hurts. I want my Daddy." Thoughts raced through my mind with jet-age speed. I needed to be with her, but it was not allowed. I was anxious about her appearance, but could do nothing about that. I wondered about the emotional scars from the trauma, but only time would reveal them. It was a time to pray, but could I when the discipline had become so meaningless?

II

Since that day the Scripture passage from Thessalonians has had a meaning that had not possessed me before. "Rejoice always, pray without ceasing, in every thing give thanks." (I Thess. 5:16-18.) I came to see prayer not as saving holy spots in each day but seeking the holy in the commonplace. It is not disengagement from the world, but radical engagement, penetration through the world to God. The words of an English bishop, J. A. T. Robinson, say it well: "My own experience is that I am really praying for people, agonizing with God for them, precisely *as* I meet them and give my soul to them. It is then if ever, in incarnational relationship, that deep speaks to deep and the Spirit of God is able to take up our inarticulate groans and turn them into prayer."[38] Prayer, then, is not turning away from others for sacred dialogue, but standing seriously and sensitively with them until the word between us becomes a word beyond us. To "pray without ceasing" is not to be forever on bended knee before some absentee divine; it is in every moment to be aware that God is met, praised, and served in our struggle with this world. To be open to another in love is to be with him in the presence of God; to struggle at the side of the Negro for his rights is to praise the God of justice; to acknowledge one's weakness and failure to another is a form of confession to a merciful God; to rejoice and be grateful in another's gift of himself is to be a recipient of the grace of God.

If we are to recover immediacy in prayer, we need to understand that we have a worldly God, One who meets us where we are. We don't have to go off somewhere alone to be with God; he is forever coming wrapped up in the moment or person at hand. That's the way Scripture sees it. Jacob came up against him while in flight from Esau, whom he had cheated of his birthright. The disciples met their Lord in the midst of fear and fright after the crucifixion. Paul encountered Christ on the Damascus road while about a hateful mission. Those who turn away from the world to find God miss him in their midst. The measure of our authenticity as Christians is not how faithfully we set aside time for God, but how sensitive we are to the sacred in the secular. To feed the hungry, to defend the oppressed, to love the unlovable, to forgive the guilty, is to be in prayerful communion with the God who is God to us in the world.

At the risk of being misunderstood, I would suggest that the discipline of prayer be set not by the clock but by the pressure of the moment. Only when we are driven to our knees can we begin to pray as men whose whole being is intensely concerned with God. And that demands greater discipline, not less. When we can't be done with God at fixed times, then we have to contend with him at all times. It would be easier otherwise, we could go about our business in the assurance that we had given divinity its due. But to know that the Holy is hidden in the depths of each moment is to pray without ceasing, to be aware that God is here and now, not then and later.

III

If we can learn that immediacy in prayer is recovered when we are alert to the presence of God where we are, perhaps we can return to what we have rejected. There is nothing inherently wrong with routine and discipline. Unless perfunctory, it is inherently right. The person who has found the beyond lodged in his midst will want and need to withdraw from the pressures and patterns of the day. He will covet moments in which he can reflect and meditate upon what has been happening between himself and God.

There will be times when we need to reflect upon his glory and majesty, his utter sublimity; to stand in awe and wonder before all he is to us and others; to revel in the world he has made for our habitation; to marvel at how wondrously he has wrought us; to rejoice in the presence of another set beside us.

There will be times when we need to bring others with us into the privacy of our communion—someone sick or lonely, someone we have wronged and with whom we seek reunion, someone whose need is beyond our meeting or strength to endure, someone from whom we are separated and long to be with.

There will be times when we need to ask for help in restraining passions of mind and body, for relief from guilt beyond our bearing, for strength to cope with anguish and with pain, for release from depression and the feeling that all is lost, for the courage to withstand temptation, for the vision to dream and hope again.

There will be times when we need to come before him in thanksgiving for common and extraordinary blessings —the simple comforts of each day, that person who has come to mean much to us, that task in which we take delight, the challenge of study and the joy of learning, the very gift of life itself.

Then ritual and routine will not be an evasion of God or his creation, but that moment which enables us to see him more clearly in the world. Then we will be able to embrace the words of Paul as our own: "Rejoice always, pray without ceasing, in every thing give thanks" (I Thess. 5:16-18).

12

Isn't One Religion as Good as Another?

The relationship of Christianity to other religions is an issue that intrigues and perplexes modern men with a new intensity now that we live in a shrunken world where direct contact is common. How are we to reconcile the diverse claims and conflicting loyalties of men with respect to what is ultimate?

Usually a pivotal word in dealing with this issue is tolerance. A man's faith is sacred; what right have we to question what he holds to be true and condemn him to hell for not believing as we do? Perhaps none. But we ought to be aware that there are two forms of tolerance. One is simple respect, a desire in no way to restrain the exercise of another's faith. That sense of the word was exemplified by a nurse in a New York hospital. One of her patients was a woman whose religion dictated that each part of her body be washed with different water. The nurse respected the patient's spiritual tradition, though it meant carrying eight or ten pans of water the length of the floor. But there is another form of tolerance. It maintains that truth is always relative to a particular person at a particular time and place. What is true for one may not be true for another. The attitude is evident in the Hindu contention that

God is one, but the ways of approach to him are many. He welcomes us along many paths, and that religious tradition is best in which we are born and bred.

This image of tolerance may well reflect our noblest impulse, but is it a responsible answer to the problem? I think not.

I

First of all, it goes on the rocks at this point: Christianity, or any other religion, cannot be true if it is not to some degree exclusive, if it does not assert itself over against what contradicts it in other faiths. Paul makes this clear in a speech to the Athenians, who were distinguished for the number of religions to which they gave hospitality. Into this context Paul came preaching "Jesus and the resurrection." Note his approach: "Men of Athens, I perceive that in every way you are very religious. For as I passed along, and observed the objects of your worship, I found also an altar with this inscription, 'To an unknown god.' What therefore you worship as unknown, this I proclaim to you." (Acts 17:22-23.) It must have sounded for a moment as if he were going to give them another religious option. But he proceeded to topple their idols and demolish their naïve syncretism. "The God who made the world and everything in it, being Lord of heaven and earth, does not live in shrines made by man." (Acts 17:24.) Paul does not for a moment suggest that we are all climbing the same mountain by equally appropriate routes. He emphatically denies that the Athenian idols are a way to the God revealed in Christ.

Here we are up against the offensiveness of truth, religious or otherwise. By its very nature it is exclusive and cannot recognize the validity of its opposite. If I were to claim that Mr. Johnson is President of the United States, and you said that Mr. Goldwater holds that office, one of us would have to be wrong. You would not think of saying that one claim was true for you and another for me because we were born and bred in it. Truth is singular, exclusive, and in this sense intolerant.

Yet this perception is one that we resist in matters religious. Many people are inclined to say that a religion is true to the extent that it is inclusive; its authenticity resides in its ability to embrace all and reject none. We are attracted to the broad-mindedness of the Hindu, who is willing to set Christ alongside others as a valid way to God. The attitude that there are few places dedicated to God in which a Hindu may not worship and few prayers in which he may not join is indeed admirable in tone.

But, implicit in this is the schizophrenic perception of truth. How can you wrap into a single bundle ultimate convictions that mutually exclude each other? Look at what you would have to reconcile: the Hindu belief in a caste system that envisages some men as created untouchables, and the Christian belief in a community where all men are of equal importance to God; the Buddhist tenet that the human self has no identity or individual significance, and the Christian tenet that coming to oneself before God is of prime importance; the Muslim conviction that a man has simply to obey religious laws to accredit himself with God, and the Christian conviction that only by the grace of God are we reconciled; the Hindu affirmation of the reincarnation of the soul until it is purified, and the Christian affirmation of the resurrection. Even a god couldn't blend those contraries. Each one precludes the possibility that the other could be true.

A minimum response to our problem, then, is the recognition that whatever religion is true must be to some de-

gree exclusive. An endlessly open mind is one closed to
the truth.

II

But then we need to go on and declare that no religion,
including Christianity, is of any significance. It is revealing
that nowhere in the New Testament is the Christian faith
called a religion and that the term is applied only twice
to Judaism. The fact is that the Bible is one long tirade
against religion: it reflects the battle between faith in the
events in which God disclosed himself and human efforts
to secure God as a weapon against the inconvenience of
life. Religion is man's effort "to connect himself with God"
that the deity might serve his purpose.

One of the earliest manifestations of this occurred in the
nation Israel. Moses had led this people out of bondage
in Egypt to the foot of Mt. Sinai. For the purpose of re-
ceiving the Ten Commandments, Moses was summoned
by God up onto the mountain. Since he was gone forty
days and forty nights, his followers were plagued with
insecurity and they inveigled his brother Aaron to "make
us gods, who shall go before us" (Ex. 32:1), who will
guarantee our well-being along the way. When he acceded
to their desire, they contributed their jewelry to be formed
into a golden calf before which they worshiped and offered
sacrifices. The people perceived this as no act of apostasy,
for they proclaimed that this was an altar to the one God.
When Moses returned, he thought otherwise. This was
nothing but an organized effort to bring God to their
terms, to possess his presence, to elevate themselves to
the realm of his protection. They were not content with
faith in a promise, but wanted to nail it down.

Now do you see what religion is, and why, as such,

Christianity is of no significance? It is the perennial effort of man by rite and ritual to assure himself of God, to guarantee his blessing. That is why Karl Barth perceives "religion as unbelief,"[39] the concern of "godless man." It's a human manufacture that has no room for faith on man's part and grace on God's; it's a wedge that man levies against the prerogatives of his creator.

That judgment cuts as deeply into Christianity as any other religion. In our religious practices we "use" God, or attempt to! We do not come to worship to offer praise and thanksgiving for the gift of life, but to "get something" that will enable us to tolerate the week ahead. We do not bring a child to Baptism as an act of dedication to God but as an inoculation, like polio shots, against the vicissitudes of life. We do not come to the Lord's Supper to submit ourselves to the judgment of God and be enfolded in his forgiveness, but as a means of shrugging off our guilt that we may do the same things again. What were intended to be acts of faith have, in fact, become acts of unbelief. They reflect the insecurity of the Israelites who induced Aaron to "make us gods, who shall go before us" (Ex. 32:1).

Therefore, we ought to invite no man to our religion, for it is of no significance; it is a reach for God rather than a response to him. In this sense one religion is as good and as false as another. No religion matters.

III

But something that has happened does and this is the crux of the matter. In the event of Christ, God has come to us, has been present in our midst, and has made known his love. Man's desire to be connected with God—a connection he can never achieve—has been established from the other side. Paul says that "God was in Christ reconciling the world unto himself" (II Cor. 5:19). Not in Buddha, not Muhammad, not in Christianity, not in philosophy and religion, but in Christ there was opened a new possibility. Paul calls it "the new creation," a new state of things in which man's desire for God is fulfilled in God's desire for man. This event is the end of religion, the cancellation of the human effort to secure God. There is now a grace in our midst available to all men. The barrier that separated them from God has been removed, the curtain raised on a new act in the drama of life.

But what relationship does Christianity have to this event? If Christians believe it to be their possession—that they have a favored position—they are of all men to be condemned. Paul does not say that in Christianity there is salvation, but that "there is salvation in no one else" than Christ (Acts 4:12). He is the way to God, or rather, God's way to us. The significance of Christianity—and its only claim on this score—is that it points away from itself to that moment of history in which God did something about the human predicament. As one theologian has phrased it, "Christianity is one beggar telling another beggar where to find food." We are people without a claim on God directing a world without a claim on God to the event in which God made a claim on all men. Christianity is without significance, but the event to which Christians witness is decisive.

What, then, do we say to the Hindu, the Muslim, the Buddhist, the Jew? Just this: Your religion is as good and as bad as ours. There is no profit in comparing theologies, spiritual heroes, codes of conduct, or even the impact of our traditions through the ages. None of this matters. One thing does: The event of Christ. In him God did something; he reconciled black and white, rich and poor, intellectual and ignoramus, sinner and saint, theist and atheist, unto himself. In him there is life, communion with God. We do not claim to have the truth but that the truth has grasped us. It was born in a manger, it hung on a cross, it broke loose from death, it lives for all men. It is the "new creation" that judges us alike and invites us alike to share in it.[40]

13

Away with the Manger

The recital of the Christmas story each year evokes in many of us rather ambivalent feelings. One portion of our thinking and feeling resonates with the sheer charm and fancy of it. The mother-and-child dimension alone strains for our appreciation. The persistence of the Wise Men and the shepherds in outwitting crafty Herod calls for admiration. Then the humbleness and the simplicity of the event work their way into our sensibilities. There is something so right about the story, we would not have a jot or tittle of it otherwise. Yet another portion of thinking and feeling begs off. The sentimentality is suffocating. The dancing stars and donkeys on bended knees before the Christ-child stretch our sense of credibility. The folklore quality invites dismissal as fantasy. At times the entire story puts distance between us and the message it would deliver. Perhaps the best way to appease our ambivalent responses is to take a vacation from the narrative on occasion. Thus I propose that we explore the meaning of Christmas through another passage of Scripture. It enables us to raise the questions and hear the affirmations without the folklore and sentimentality.

John the Baptist, who perceived himself as a forerunner of the Messiah, had been cast into prison by Herod

Antipas. For reasons that we do not know, his thoughts
focused on One whom he had earlier baptized and whom
some were now acclaiming as the Messiah. John then
sent two of his own disciples to Jesus with the question,
"Are you he who is to come, or shall we look for another?" Jesus replied, "Go and tell John what you hear
and see: the blind receive their sight and the lame walk,
lepers are cleansed and the deaf hear, and the dead are
raised up, and the poor have good news preached to them"
(Matt. 11:2-6).

After reading this, many feel, I suspect, as offended as
by the familiar Christmas folklore. For one thing, we do
not perceive ourselves as asking the same question. Who
among us feels himself to be a part of a community
desperately awaiting a Messiah? John's concern is mounted
on a long-standing expectation apparently not our own.
Israel's hope in the coming of a Messiah, a king who
would bring an end to injustice and evil, establish a kingdom of righteousness and peace, is simply extraneous to
our thought world. And so we readily dismiss the question,
"Are you he who is to come . . . ?" (Matt. 11:3). It may
reach back to David, find dramatic accent in the prophets,
and stalk the mentality of every faithful Jew, but it does
not extend itself into our lives.

And in all honesty we can be no more hospitable to the
answer Jesus gives. In it he lays claim to descriptions of
the Messiah in two passages of Isaiah as a means of
identifying himself. That would hone the edge of the hopes
and dreams of every Jew, but it can only blunt ours. We
are not Jews and do not share their messianic imagery.
If the whole of the Old Testament had been brought forward to focus on the event of Christ, we would not be
moved. Thus it seems that our Scripture passage presents
us with a question we do not have and an answer we

cannot accept. And if anything, we crave to be back with the manger scene where we are at least charmed.

I

But I wonder if John's question is really so foreign to our existence. Can we deny that a residual discontent drifts one day and rushes another through our lives? that constraining and unattractive alternatives present themselves to us day by day? that turns of fate leave us feeling like a victim of circumstance? When we are in touch with these feelings, from underneath them there emerges a question that is but a secular version of John's: Is there a new possibility for my life, can someone or something make it different? We may not be in hot pursuit of a Messiah, but every fiber of our being cries out for deliverance from the present state of things. And we would echo the cry of Eugene O'Neill's character in *Days Without End:* "A new saviour must be born . . . so that we can be free from the past and inherit the future."

Here is a person with inner anguish, torn and tortured by forces over which he has no control. In his every mood and movement he knows himself to be a victim, wrenched in one direction and another by something not of his choosing. And from deep within himself the question comes, Can I be set free of this bondage for spontaneous responses? Here is another person for whom the future is a constant threat. The past has been in such forms as to undermine his confidence, and the future he perceives as permeated by capriciousness and deceit. Buried in his anxiety about tomorrow is the question: Is there something upon which I can pin my hopes? Or again, here is another person for whom meaning is always a question and never an answer. He goes through the

motions of existence but can find no purpose or significance in it. There are just actions and reactions with no
thread weaving them into a pattern. Late in the night and
early in the morning he is obsessed with thoughts of giving up what he is doing. And hidden in his emptiness is
the question, Can there be any meaning to my existence?

Each of the questions is a secularized form of John the
Baptist's inquiry. We may not ask of the Christ if he is
the one to come, but we ask if someone or something can
give new possibilities to our lives. For the Baptist it is the
question of Christmas, for us it is the question raised by
our existence. Every facet of our being cries out for newness.

II

Now what of the answer Jesus gives? To the messenger
he said, "Go and tell John what you hear and see: the
blind receive their sight and the lame walk, lepers are
cleansed and the deaf hear, and the dead are raised up,
and the poor have good news preached to them" (Matt.
11:4-5). Few of us are impressed by the parallel between
these words and the messianic descriptions in Isaiah. The
fact is that if we saw and heard the same things, we would
impose a different interpretation. If the blind receive their
sight and the lame walk, it is the result of a surgeon's
skill; if the deaf hear, it is by virtue of a mechanical de-
vice magnifying sound in the ear; if the dead return to life,
it is by massaging the heart until it beats again; and if
good news is preached to the poor, it is the voice of a
welfare agency. Thus we imply fraud at the heart of our
story.

But now forget the surface ambiguities, look and listen
around the edges of this response, see and hear the mes-

sage behind it. Jesus is identifying himself as the bearer of new possibilities in human existence. Because he has come, things can be different. What is it that he brings, what is it that makes all things new? It is not a law by which to guide our behavior, we have more than we can obey, as it is; it is not a philosophy of life, we have more of them than we can use; and it is not another ritual by which to evidence our faith, we would as soon have fewer of them. What comes to us in Christ, never made quite as explicit and unequivocable before, is the realization that God is unalterably and recklessly *for* man. At the very heart of his Being is the determination to affirm our authentic existence, to confirm in every way our essential humanity. What gives new possibilities is a God whose only will for us is that our lives be all they can be. Thus when Paul wants to identify the meaning of the Christ event, he speaks of "a new being," "a new creation," "a new state of things."

We must ask whether this newness has been in our midst, whether the new possibilities promised in Christ have been fulfilled in our lives. If there has been a moment in which you were grasped by a human face as human, forgetting its color, the beauty or ugliness of its features, the differences of age, strength, and knowledge, then you have experienced "the new being." If there has been a moment in which you could claim your parents or your children through all they have done to displease and distort you, then you have participated in "a new creation." If there has been a moment in which you have become aware of the perversity within your heart yet have found a deeper self-acceptance, then you have been a part of "the new reality." If there has been a moment in which you have set aside your own needs long enough to share another's, then you have known "a new state of things." If there has been a moment in which the past ceased to confine you and the future to frighten you, then you have experienced "the new being."

When any of these moments were yours, they were evidence that newness promised in the coming of Christ became real in your life. If you cannot call these experiences by the same name given them by Christians, do not try. Perhaps that will come later, perhaps it will never come, perhaps it is not important! The only ultimate demand is that you be open to the newness, "accept it, enter into it, let it grasp you."[41] For now, at least, do not be bothered that others call it the presence of God.

"Are you he who is to come . . . ?" is at once the question of the Messiah and the question of existence. For those of us uncomfortable with the vocabulary of faith, it can be translated, "Is there a new possibility for my life?" And the reply of Jesus, "Go and tell John what you see and hear" is at once the answer of faith and the fulfillment of the deepest need within each of us. If you cannot accept the form in which faith gives this answer, translate it into the newness you have found in your own existence.

But then allow others to see this question and answer as the meaning of the Christmas event. We will join you with the need to do away with the manger, with the baby Jesus mystique, with the stars dancing in the skies and donkeys on bended knees before the Christ-child. Yet at the Christmas season you are invited to celebrate the newness each of us has found by joining in one mighty chorus around the globe singing, "Glory to God in the highest . . ."

14

Raising Modern Christians

Over the years I have listened rather cynically to the contention of young people that they will raise their children differently from the way they themselves were raised. Perhaps this is because as a parent I have done and said most of the things I swore I never would. But there is one point at which I am inclined to believe them. It was focused one day when a group of them argued that the one thing they would never do was send their children to Sunday school. Now I suspect they will; the prospect of having someone else distract our youngsters for several hours for a nominal donation is more than most of us can resist. But that is not the real issue. Behind the protest was the feeling that they had been exposed to superstition and sentimentality in a degree which now made the Christian faith unattractive. Aside from a few memorable hayrides in the senior high fellowship, the experience had been disillusioning in the context of what they learned in college. Of course, some would argue that rejecting religion in college is a phase everyone goes through. In a sense it is. But there is a chance this generation won't come out of it. I have a strong hunch that many of them will be "hung up" on religion the rest of their lives. The burden this casts upon

parents is that of nurturing a faith which can withstand
the complexities of the age in which we live.

I

Now if we are to raise modern Christians, I think it
is important to talk as little as possible in religious terms.
They have no meaningful frame of reference to the child
at the time and often become the source of distortion
later. The kind of dialogue I have in mind is this: The
child asks who made the world, and we respond that
"God created the world"; the child asks where God lives,
and we say "up there"; the child asks why he should be
good, and we answer because "God is watching you."
These responses may be uncomfortably familiar to some
and even creditable to others, but they are usually ineffective on two counts. For one thing, the question
seldom means to us what it does to the child. As often
as not we answer a question he isn't asking. And then
the richness of meaning in a religious assertion is usually
inaccessible to a child. His capacity for abstraction and
conceptualization is not yet developed. The other day my
four-year-old daughter threw back her blond hair, flashed
her blue eyes as only a daughter can at her father, and
asked, "Daddy, is God dead?" My first impulse was to
pontificate in some detail upon the new theology, my
second was to make some pious references to eternity, and
the third, upon which I acted, was to say, "No." While
the latter response may reveal some lack of imagination,
it was the least inadequate of the three. But they all
misread the question. Knowing that my daughter had had
several recent experiences of death, I should have recognized that she was asking if it was as real and final as it
appeared to be. Her concern was solely to grasp the

nature of death; God merely served as an object to which it could happen. Had I responded to her in terms of his eternity or immortality, I would not only have missed her question but have confused her with an abstraction she had no way of comprehending. There is no possibility that a religious term could mean anything to her. Parents will do the Christian faith the greatest service by disciplining themselves to avoid religious verbiage.

But the positive dimension of our responsibility is to nurture children in experiences that can later facilitate religious understanding. It is crucial that we begin with life, not creedal explanations of it. Perhaps we need to be reminded that this is the way the Judeo-Christian faith emerged. Its symbols and dogmas were not created in advance of experiences but as interpretations of them. For example, the people of Israel called God their Deliverer. But that image was rooted in the experience of the exodus where they had been delivered from bondage to the Egyptians. All the rhetoric and ritual that followed were a means of celebrating and reminding themselves of its truth. If we are to be effective in nurturing children in that faith, we must first concentrate upon the experiences and let the religious terminology come later.

Let me be specific. I am concerned that children have every possible experience of awe, wonder, mystery, and amazement. These feelings may come as children are exposed to a phenomenon of nature, as they listen to a children's concert, or as they watch a newborn baby. Later they will have categories for grasping the nature of God. I am concerned that children experience the brutality between man and man. They ought not to be protected from the cruelty and misery of war, the tensions between their parents, and those hurtful words they inflict upon each other. Later it will enable them to understand the

sinful nature of man. I am concerned that they experience
the undeservedness of existence, the feeling they have
been given what they did not earn, that they have been
cared for when they had nothing to contribute. Later the
grace of God will have analogues through which it can
be grasped. I am concerned that they experience the
responsibility to bear the burdens of others, to weep and
rejoice with them, and to endure whatever share of suffering that identification demands. Later it will help them
understand the cross of Christ and the demands it makes
upon us. Our task is simply to provide and nurture these
experiences in ways that are real and in places that are
natural. To divert them into religious categories is an
adult exercise for which they are not ready. When the
time comes to function with symbols and dogmas, our
children will have an abundant supply of experience to
draw upon.

II

Now there is a vehicle of understanding that is acces-
sible to persons at any age. It is the story, the "once upon
a time" world in which a child lives so fully. From it he
can grasp feelings and meanings that later can be expressed in religious assertions.

This suggests that in raising modern Christians we can
immerse children in Biblical narratives. Often their raw
imagination can interact with them more freely and deeply
than we can. But there is an issue here that must be faced
head on: the subtle distinction between fact and myth,
between historical occurrence and the message or meaning. This distinction is not easily made, much less com-
municated, but let me suggest one instance in which it
can be made clear. When my daughters ask me how the

world came to be, I intend to respond on two levels. The first is that of scientific explanation. In a rather crude way we will talk about evolution as one thing developing out of another. Experientially the closest a child can come to understanding this is through planting a seed and having a flower come later. Obviously that is not evolution, but it is analogous and will enable her to understand that there are stages and processes in the creation of the world. The other level at which we will examine her question is through the Biblical story of creation. Here the focus is upon who we are in relation to God, the world, and one another. It is not concerned really with how we got here but how we live here. There are many dimensions to this parabolic narrative, but one for which the child has an experiential referent is that man is God's helper in the world and he has special responsibility to look after things. I might explain it this way to my daughter: "Sara, when you plant your garden, you are helping God make the world more beautiful; when you take your sister's hand to cross the street, you are helping God protect her; when you set and clear the table for your mother, you are helping God make her work easier."

If we hold the two explanations side by side, we need never fear that children will confuse fact and interpretation, that what they will learn in school will contradict what they understand to be the Christian position. And I think we need not fear that anything of the wonder and delight of the stories will be lost. Nothing is destroyed for the child when he understands that Sleeping Beauty was not a real princess, that the Emperor did not really walk in the procession without his clothes, or that Robin Hood did not rob the rich to help the poor. A story does not need to be historical to be real.

But having argued that we can use Biblical narratives,

I want to set a ground rule: We ought to limit ourselves to those which tie in with something the child knows to be real. It once was argued that we could tell him any Biblical story and in time he would come upon the experiences with which to understand it. But it never quite happened for many; that's why we have a generation of students now protesting that religion is irrelevant. The stories of faith were never bound to real experiences in their lives. The wife of Bishop Robinson provides an illustration of relating a narrative and its meaning in terms of experience. She had been talking with her children about Jesus and in particular about the story of how he healed Peter's mother-in-law. From this they might have been led to think of Jesus as a magician or at least a figure about whom increditable legends arose. But in this instance one child tied it in with something she knew to be true in her own experience. "I expect she [the mother-in-law] was so fed up because Peter had been spending much time wandering about Galilee with Jesus instead of looking after her daughter that she had a temperature and went to bed. And it was only when Jesus himself came to the house and she saw what sort of person he was that she wanted to get up and do things for other people."[42] The child had grasped the kind of change that can come over someone who is feeling resentful when a gesture of love happens to him and creates the desire to do something for others. For her that story will never be irrelevant nor her understanding of Jesus superstitious; neither will anything she learns in college cause her to reject it.

In the book of Deuteronomy the author defines the great commandment: "The LORD our God is one LORD; and you shall love the LORD your God with all your heart, and with all your soul, and with all your might." Then he says, "And these words which I command you this day shall be upon your heart; and you shall teach them diligently to your children, and shall talk of them when you sit in your house" (Deut. 6:4-7). That charge is neither easy nor comfortable. It never has been. Perhaps the times in which we find ourselves make it even more difficult. But the faith we are called upon to share is durable. And the God in whom we believe can be trusted beyond our frailties.

PART THREE

ASSUMING A CHRISTIAN PERSPECTIVE

15
The Responsible Person

The responses people make to the events of the day have a way of reflecting the ethic of the age. An incident several summers ago provides a case in point. Taking his clue from the Continent, a San Francisco designer introduced the topless bathing suit for women. Not to be outdone, a Los Angeles designer amplified the top and brought forth a bottomless suit. (At the time it occurred to me that if the two designers joined forces, it would depress the industry!) While clergymen sputtered moral platitudes, little old ladies in tennis shoes registered shock, and the average male took off for the public beaches, these revealing comments were made by two Hollywood actresses. Debbie Reynolds said she couldn't see anything wrong with exposing oneself; she just couldn't imagine herself doing it. Mamie Van Doren, on the other hand, thought the topless suit appropriate around one's own pool and among friends. Their responses have one thing in common: They are expressions of the privativistic ethic, the assumption that the individual is the ultimate and autonomous arbiter of moral issues. The categories of freedom and responsibility, right and wrong, honor and integrity, are conspicuous by their absence. Conduct is only subject to the taste and disposition of the individual.

Although the privativistic ethic is an ancient creed, its advocacy has become more intense and practice more common. A deal once considered questionable is now perceived as shrewd; to break the rules of a community and not get caught is evidence of merit; the sowing of wild oats is a right and obligation for the maturing male (though not his female counterpart). Thus morals are a private affair; as long as you can live with yourself, nothing else matters. Against this vision let us explore what it means to be a responsible person.

Our first task is always to identify the context within which decisions are to be made. Many would direct our attention to eternal and unchanging laws. Some things are always right, others always wrong. The moral person is the one who knows the rules and obeys them. And the task of ethics is to catalog the regulations for behavior, to expound an exhaustive system which with corollaries is adaptable to all the varieties of life. As a youngster I caught the spirit of that and set myself to an arduous task. I determined to read through the Bible and select all its legislations for behavior. About a third of the way through Genesis, I got bored and decided to risk playing things by ear! To live by external legislation has never appealed to me since. I suspect it is meaningless to you.

The New Testament as I understand it directs us away

from what some have called "the sanctions of Mt. Sinai"
and "the clear teachings of our Lord." It demands that
we begin in that moment when person must contend with
person in all their uniqueness; it summons us in the
particularity of a given situation to take seriously the
humanness of others. The thing that matters is not the
application of principles, but the confirmation of personhood. Let this incident provide the clue. Jesus had been
invited by Simon, a Pharisee, to a banquet in his honor.
The pristine purity of the occasion was violated in the
eyes of the host when a prostitute came into the dining
room, knelt before Jesus, anointed his feet with her tears
and dried them with her hair. It was for her an act of
repentance. Simon had a rule that defined her as immoral
and he rejected her. But Jesus responded to the person,
to the depths that were evident within her. Turning to
Simon he said, "Do you see this woman?" (Luke 7:44),
"Do you see here a human being?"

What I am suggesting is that our decisions begin in an
intense sensitivity to what is happening within and between persons. The only moral imperative is to react so
that the honor and integrity of each are maintained. And
in the last resort, persons are more demanding than principles. They require that we search out ourselves and
others until in a given moment we respond from the
depths of love. The responsible person is one who knows
the haunting demands of being a person and preserving
the personhood of others.

That may sound humanistic, it is; it may appear to be
a denial of revelation, it is not. God does not make his
claim upon us through rules and regulations; he did not
send his Son as a professor of ethics with celestial degrees. Jesus entered through the stable door of ordinary
experience and in man-to-man encounter made his claim.

And the claim was this: to be humanizing in our relationships, to affirm one another in the worth and dignity he
holds us. It's a strangely Christian thing Albert Camus
puts on the lips of Dr. Rieux in *The Plague:* "Heroism
and sanctity don't really appeal to me. . . . What interests
me is being a man."[43]

II

But while the responsible person begins within the
situation at hand, he operates between the poles of "fixity
and freedom." At the risk of appearing to contradict what
has been said, we must establish the place of ethical
admonitions and prohibitions. We don't need to be told
that the Bible is full of them; they have been thrown up
at us from childhood. We do need to gain perspective on
them.

Now it ought to be understood that Jesus never intended his teachings to be frozen into laws binding upon
men in every moment. His words were occasional, spoken
for a moment, illustrative of what love might demand at
a given time. To treat them as elastic, stretchable to en-
gulf every future situation, is to distort them. Jesus spoke
"of God and of men and of the human community in a
relational and living fashion, and . . . in the course of his
speech . . . [swept] down now here, now there; . . . [picked]
up some detail, situation, instance of human pathos, error,
pride, . . . [and held] it up for a moment, and then moved
on."[44]

Yet even that does not account for apparent absolutes.
Scripture, old and new alike, lays down stern demands
from time to time. We cannot rationalize away its prohibi-
tion of killing, the boundaries it sets for sex, its demand
for honor in human affairs. What is the function of these

formulated laws? Are they absolutely binding? Paul Tillich provides a clue: "They represent the wisdom of the
past about man, his relations to others and himself, his
predicament in temporal existence, and the *telos* or inner
aim of his being. . . . They guide the conscience in con-
crete situations."[45] Without claiming absolute validity, they
give concretion to the demands of love; as progenitors of
moral habit, they are the guides and aides in the making
of decisions. Through the ages they have taken on an
authority that we violate with risk and accept without question at our peril.

Thus freedom is the polar counterpart of fixity. In the
moment of choice man is called upon to improvise, to
interpret what love may require of him in a particular
situation. The Christian ethic does not say that there is
never a moment in which the taking of another's life is an
option, that sex within marriage is always honorable and
outside always illicit, that a word falsely spoken is blasphemous at any time. What is demanded in one moment
is not demanded in another. Love has as many ways as
there are persons and situations. And you have the terrible freedom to decide what love requires of you, re-
specting fixity yet never tyrannized by it. For all the risk
in improvising, the simple fact is that life is too ambiguous,
man too noble, and love too creative for it to be otherwise.

III

We have said that the responsible person takes as his
starting point the immediacy of person-to-person encounter and that he brackets it with freedom and fixity.
But there is another dimension into which we must gather
up what has been said. In any moment of decision we

are responding to some action upon us. It may be what another has done to me, and I return in kind; it may be what the culture defines as prudent, and I yield to its authority; or it may be the expectation someone has of me, and I sacrifice my own inclination. Thus action is reaction, response to something that has happened to us. And what separates the responsible from the irresponsible person is that to which he chooses to respond.

It is at this point that the Christian message becomes acutely relevant. In personal confession, Paul gives us a charter: "It is no longer I who live, but Christ who lives in me; and the life I now live in the flesh I live by faith in the Son of God, who loved me and gave himself for me" (Gal. 2:20). There is much in this statement which is foreign and offensive, but let it be said this way: In each moment of decision I strive to live in response to what God has done in Christ. In this man God acted in a humanizing way; every word and deed was calculated to confirm the integrity and depth of personhood. He touched the core of life until it became the crown. In the tax collector he confirmed the passion to be accepted; in the prostitute he honored her desire to be free of her past; in the sick he nourished the mind and body in their struggle for health; in the lonely and rejected he opened the way to relationship; in the hopeless and depressed he strengthened the will to meaning. Jesus did the humanizing thing to persons until they recovered what they were meant to be.

At risk of being misunderstood, it could be said that the Christian is called to "faithful reenactments" of the life of Christ. This doesn't mean that in him we have the blueprint for behavior. He never faced many of the problems we do. But it does mean that in our moment of decision we choose as the object of our response the one who loved us and gave himself for the recovery of personhood. Then the boundaries of sexual exploration between a man and woman are not set by rule or passion; then the life we live in our communities is not set by prevailing ethos; then the responses we make to the actions of others are not set by custom or revenge; then our honor and integrity is not defined by what we can get away with or what the law demands; the center of response is the humanizing way of God with man in Christ.

If that becomes for us a style of life, we can say with Paul, "It is no longer I who live, but Christ who lives in me" (Gal. 2:20). The responsible person is the one in whom Christ lives again.

16

The Warm, Dry Handshake

Many of us have found ourselves among an unprece-
dented gathering. What brought us together was more
intoxicating than beer, more palm-perspiring than a space-
ship on the launching pad, and more mysterious than the
way teachers determine grades. The attraction was James
Bond, that intriguing secret agent who has been charac-
terized as the man with "the warm, dry handshake."
Many of us are now prepared to return Charlie Brown
and Peanuts to the adolescents, to sign over our *Playboy*
subscription to those of a more puritanical bent, and to
leave the "tiger in your tank" to little old ladies in sports
cars. We have found a hero.

One of the favorite pastimes of those who take the fun
out of everything by analyzing it is the attempt to identify
why Agent 007 has become "the biggest mass-cult hero
of the decade." Some suggest that the addiction is formed
by the fiendish ingenuity of Ian Fleming. Where else
could one find a chauffeur like Goldfinger's who can slit
a throat with a flip of his steel derby, poison-tipped spikes
that can be projected from the soles of shoes, and a pistol
concealed in a large volume of *The Bible to Be Read as
Literature*? In *Thunderball*, Bond escapes his captors by
diving off a balcony only to be propelled through space

by his jet-powered backpack. There's something for the man who has everything!

Others have contended that our fascination with 007 centers on his inordinate success as a lover. His instant attractiveness and adroit technique are an inspiration to lesser men. In each of the thirteen Bond books there is one woman upon whom our hero concentrates. Out of the thirteen he manages to seduce eleven—not a bad average in any league! You may recall one of the exceptions in *Goldfinger*—Tilly Masterson. Bond attributes his failure to the fact that she "was one of those girls whose hormones got mixed up . . . a direct consequence of giving votes to women."[46] There is an innovation in *Thunderball*—underwater sex. But it is subtle: All that the cameras show are bubbles merging by a reef.

I am not concerned with why we are afflicted with Bondomania, but with what this modern folk hero says to us about ourselves. It may come as a surprise, but Ian Fleming is a writer of intensely serious purpose. He perceives himself as a moral exorcist who would purge us of our illusions and distortions. In reflecting upon his mission, Fleming tells us that he is concerned to expose seven modern sins which are deadlier than their ancient counterparts. He identifies them as Avarice, Cruelty, Snobbery, Hypocrisy, Self-righteousness, Moral Cowardice, and Malice. Far from glorifying the "sex, sadism, and snobbery" so evident in his works, he is holding them up to ridicule. The weight of his convictions is in this hypothesis: "If I were to put these modern seven into the scales against the ancient seven I cannot but feel that the weight of the former would bring the brass tray crashing down. . . . As a man in the street, I can only express my belief that being possessed of the ancient seven deadly sins one can still go to heaven, whereas to be afflicted by the modern variations can only be a passport to hell."[47]

While in the movie versions it appears that his intent is to make us laugh, it is in fact to make us weep—weep over what we see of ourselves in James Bond. Agent 007 is an image—drawn in grotesque proportions to be sure—of modern man.

I

The first thing to which I call attention is that Bond lacks what William James called "a constructive passion of some kind." He is man without a vision or mission worthy of his life. At best he lives on the surface with all the cheap thrills and phony fulfillments that cluster there. Bond flees from moment to moment without any overriding purpose or integrating theme. Strip away the dash and daring, the elegant tastes, the double bourbons, the warm, dry handshake, and you have T. S. Eliot's "hollow man" personified—"Shape without form, Shade without colour, . . . Gesture without motion."[48]

This is not to suggest that there are no values by which he lives. Explicitly or implicitly we all have them. But each is a desire without depth, a dream without dignity, and each diminishes him as a person. Bond is loyal to M and the secret service, but his allegiance is blind and uncritical. An order to kill is received as if sanctioned by the gods. On occasion Bond seeks the companionship of others in adventure but appears to have no feeling for them. When a flamethrower burns Quadral to a crisp in *Doctor No,* he blithely steps aside and struts on to meet the enemy. Bond covets the presence of women but avoids sensitivity to their deeper needs and respect for their person. He discards his conquests like paper cups. His values are no more than a useless passion that preclude his securing himself to any of "the redeeming facts of life." For all the surface glory and excitement, he is a shadowy figure without the substance of humanity.

And I believe Ian Fleming wants us to see him as the ruins of manhood. Lest we miss the point, in the next to the last epic Fleming pictures Bond as a dissipated and disintegrated figure. We see him drinking more and eating less, sleeping fitfully and addicted to pills, sitting on a park bench sweating profusely and speculating on the carefree life of an ant. From time to time he is rejuvenated by a sports car or a pretty woman, but neither can sustain him. And at the end Bond is living in obscurity on a Japanese island, his memory gone; discharged from the service, he is being cared for by a devoted maiden skin diver. But the irony of it is that he can neither use nor enjoy her; he simply needs her to exist. Danger can no longer excite him, bourbon can no longer soothe him, women can no longer challenge him. The agent with the warm, dry handshake is now exposed for what he has always been—a hollow man, "Shape without form, Shade without colour, . . . Gesture without motion."

The late Richard Niebuhr used to say that to be a human self is to rely on something meaning-giving; to live, to love, if need be to die by a loyalty that can give substance to your existence. Without it life will be neither orderly nor meaningful but simply lost in moment-by-moment living. Through the James Bond saga, Fleming wants us to see the vacuity of our lives when they are not marshalled by "a constructive passion of some kind." It's his way of asking this generation, "For what are you living?"

II

Now the second thing to which I call attention is that James Bond lacks a moral frame of reference, a scheme or orientation within which his decisions can be made. The man is void of moral sensitivity. He kills without remorse, makes love without commitment, spends life without replenishing it. To be sure, 007 has a few scruples and aversions. He puts a high premium on loyalty to his profession, courage in the face of danger, and perseverance in the presence of the impossible. At the same time he is offended by the unscrupulous pursuit of money in *Goldfinger,* the indiscriminate violence in *Doctor No,* and the degrading tyranny in *To Russia with Love.* But a few virtues and as many aversions do not make for an ethical stance or a responsible person. The self is always constituted by its decisions, but Bond destroys himself by his.

The moral bankruptcy of the man is revealed in his easy conscience and when that fails in the rationalization that he is only doing his job. Listen to the opening lines in *Goldfinger:*

> James Bond, with two double bourbons inside him, sat in the final departure lounge of Miami Airport and thought about life and death.
> It was part of his profession to kill people. He had never liked doing it and when he had to kill he did it as well as he knew how and forgot about it. As a secret agent who held the rare double-O prefix— the licence to kill in the Secret Service—it was his duty to be as cool about death as a surgeon. If it happened, it happened. Regret was unprofessional.[49]

Tyrannized by this sense of duty, Bond dismisses the categories of right and wrong, divests himself of inner sensitivity, and hardens himself against the claims of another person. He operates in a moral vacuum.

Now Ian Fleming is certainly aware that life is too complex to be ordered by anything so simplistic as the Golden Rule or the Ten Commandments. They may be guideposts by which we find our way, but they are not hitching posts by which we can secure ourselves. More is relative than most of us have the courage to admit. The traditional props have been kicked out from under us and the social controls have been removed. Morally we are alone; the solitude and solemnity of our lives is frightening. But that is where we find ourselves and that is the beginning of responsibility. James Bond may have been able to dismiss the ethical dimension with the glib assertion that it was his job. But Fleming wants us to understand that the issue is not your job but your life, your existence as a person. And he challenges us through the moral bankruptcy of 007 to find an ethical frame of reference by which we may constitute ourselves as human beings. You weren't born human, never think you were; you become human by the decisions you make. And by those same decisions you fulfill or diminish the humanness of others. That freedom may be frightening, but the person who tries to escape it is no person at all; he's nothing but a silly figure on the face of the earth who may for a moment intrigue us, as does James Bond, but for whom we can only have pity.

Now Ian Fleming is not a theologian; nor are his writings Scripture. Yet he has a faculty for raising the right questions that reach out for a Christian response. One is reminded of Isaiah: "By men of strange lips and with alien tongue the LORD will speak to this people" (Isa. 28:11). I have no doubt that God may be speaking to us through so strange a pen as Ian Fleming's and so alien a figure as James Bond. For me the Word of God focuses on two questions, simple questions but with a depth the ages have not plumbed, and neither will you: "For what are you living?" And, "Morally, how do you make your decisions?"

17

In the Beginning Is Relation

In Arthur Miller's movie *The Misfits,* there is a scene in which Roslyn, played by Marilyn Monroe, is rehearsing the reasons she will give in order to secure a divorce. The lines have been prepared by Isabelle, a sixtyish woman who has made a career of helping others terminate their marriages. The two enact the scene soon to be played in the courtroom.

> ISABELLE: " 'Did your husband, Mr. Raymond Taber, act toward you with cruelty?' "
>
> ROSLYN: "Well, . . . yes."
>
> ISABELLE: " 'In what ways did his cruelty manifest itself?' "
>
> ROSLYN: "He . . . How's it go again?"
>
> ISABELLE: " 'He persistently and cruelly ignored my personal rights and wishes, and resorted on several occasions to physical violence against me.' "
>
> ROSLYN: "He persistently . . ." She breaks off, troubled. "Must I say that? Why can't I just say he wasn't there. I mean, you could touch him but he wasn't there."[50]

Here is a recurring theme in Miller's plays, perhaps the story of his life: In a sea of routine, people do not mean much to one another. With clammy hands and cold hearts they grasp for each other in fear of living alone; they grace each other with verbal niceties to escape or conceal their real feeling. We have experienced that, have we not? It may have been in a moment when you were about to break at the seams and could find no one to tell; when you were with another and suddenly realized you were like two deaf men talking; when you found yourself feeling strange and uncomfortable among familiar faces. It was the hell of being unable to relate meaningfully. This leads me to examine now the dynamics of a real relationship, of closeness to another person.

I

Strange as it may seem, intimacy begins with distance, accepting the "otherness" of another. If I am to be close to someone, I must be willing to see him as different from myself, to confirm the distinctiveness of his existence. You may have had the experience of liking someone who at first you disliked intensely. For that there can be many reasons, but often one is this: Your relationship began with the immediate recognition that you were different from each other. At first it was threatening and uncomfortable, but later a thing of joy. With the recognition that you were you and he was he, you could grow in respect and mutuality. The acknowledgment of distance enabled you to be close.

The opposite of this, of course, is the person who imposes his personality and thoughts upon others. In an argument where you are poles apart, he claims you are really saying the same thing in different ways. When a deep and frightening experience is shared, he intrudes what it means to him, saying that it's not really as bad as you make it. If you seek his counsel, he immediately gives advice that may be right but for which you are not ready. When you attempt to explain yourself to him, he reconstructs the image until it is a pale reflection of himself. He never treats you as a separate person, but as an extension of himself.

The psychiatrist with whom I trained in counseling writes of an incident at once simple and profound. It happened at a lunch counter in New York City. An older sister and a mother had given their orders to the waitress, who then turned to the little brother and said, "Young man, what will you have?" Before he could respond, the sister said, "I'll order for him." When the waitress again directed the question to the youngster, the mother replied, "I'll order for him." Undaunted, the waitress said a third time, "Young man, what will you have?" Somewhat timidly he said, "A hamburger." "And how would you like it—rare, medium, or well done?" With a bit more assurance he said, "Well done, please." "And what would you like on it—mustard, pickles, onions, relish, or catsup?" With growing appreciation of himself for the respect shown by another he said, "The whole works." As the waitress walked away the lad turned to his mother and said, "Gee, Mommy, she thinks I am real."[51]

Nothing is so meaningful as having another take you with that kind of seriousness, recognize and confirm your distinctiveness. Every relationship of intimacy begins with and sustains the distance between persons.

II

When this is a reality, a second thing is possible—the disclosure of oneself to another, trusting someone else with much of what one knows about one's own self. We can risk sharing ourselves with another when we trust he will not smother us with his own needs, when we know he can come close yet keep his distance. But we ought not to speak of this as if revealing oneself were second nature and happened without strain. The simple fact is that there are impulses within me I refuse to admit even to myself, there are thoughts I deny as if they were another's, there are dispositions and propensities I agonize to suppress. And nothing is more frightening than the possibility that they might escape before a public. Thus each person struggles to conceal and camouflage his real self lest he be criticized and hurt. In hiding we feel safe.

But this is not the way of health and growth. The person who keeps himself to himself soon loses himself; he evaporates before his own inward stare. It is disclosure of oneself to another that puts us in touch with our own needs and feelings enabling us to cope with them, that makes us aware of our values and enables us to examine them, that frees us to expand ourselves in new directions. No one of us can be himself unless he trusts himself to another.

This leads me to suggest a new dimension in the word "love." It is the phenomenon of knowing another and being known by him. If I love someone, I want to know his hopes and frustrations, his fears and his trusts, his talents and his limitations, his affections and his dislikes; and I display my love for him and enable him to love me by letting him know these things about me. Thus love is opening oneself to another in trust and being receptive to his self-disclosure. There's great risk in that, for the person who knows us knows where to hurt us. That's why lovers and close friends can wound each other so deeply; it's why many of us are afraid to love. But without the risk of sharing ourselves, none of us can become ourselves.

Yet disclosing oneself does not mean talking about oneself indiscriminately. The total loss of privacy is destructive. Sometimes our health and growth depend upon the strength to keep some things to ourselves. Those who ventilate every thought and feeling destroy their sense of self. This is why in every true relationship there must be times of silence. When my wife and I were dating—more years ago than we care to admit, for love struggles to hold all that is joyful in the present—she used to say, "It's the silence I love, the times we are together and no words are spoken." I think she meant in part that these were moments in which each solidified himself, recognized the boundaries of sharing, the moments in which each preserved a bit of selfhood for himself.

Thus intimacy begins with the recognition of distance and though it is fulfilled in the sharing of oneself with another, it sustains some privacy lest personhood be lost.

III

Now we must set our relationships in a theological perspective. The author of Genesis depicts the apex of creation with these words, "So God created man in his own image, in the image of God he created him" (Gen. 1:27). Scholars tangle over the meaning of "image," but one whom we can trust, Gerhard von Rad, claims that it is best understood as "resemblance."[52] Without saying that man is a god, the Bible claims that he is like God. In the midst of his creation the Creator has set one who bears a striking similarity to himself.

This gives us two clues about ourselves. First, as men

created in the image of God we are intended for relationship. At the core of divinity is the determination not to be alone but to have mutuality with man. Evidence of that begins in the creation of a being capable of responding, it permeates the life of Israel and the call of her prophets, it reaches its climax in the event of Christ. God is not God for himself, but for another; every word and deed is calculated to draw man into relation. And our resemblance to him is in this: we were created to respond and react, to enter deeply and meaningfully into the existence of others. Martin Buber has expressed this with the phrase, "In the beginning is relation"; this is what is intended for us and what we are intended for. Thus our discussion of relatedness is an elaboration of the purpose God has for man. And the person who seeks meaningful communion and mutuality with another is fulfilling not only himself but his destiny as well.

Secondly, the man who images God in relating to others finds their encounter translucent. When two persons stand before each other in openness and honor, the very Ground of All Being is exposed between them. Man in the image of God means that in his relationships he can mirror the Eternal. In the words of Martin Buber, God is the reality "between man and man"; he is real to us when we are real to each other. God is known where men know each other in trust and expectation. One evening I sat on our porch with a gentleman I had not known before and with whom I had little in common. He had not finished high school, I had graduate degrees; he was the grandfather of eight, I the father of two; he worked in a factory, I at a college. The differences were legion, but there emerged between us a determination to know each other, to understand our different worlds, to be together in trust and openness. We had been strangers brought together by circumstances, but when he left he said: "We must come together again. This has been real." I think I know what he meant: In being real with one another we had been visited by Reality, the God who is known when men know one another. "In the beginning is relation"—and at the end as well.

18

The Neighbor Is a Negro

There was a time when it seemed profitable to argue our prejudices on an abstract level where our particular emotional involvements are dormant. But prejudices are essentially emotional and not affected by rational discourse. It is virtually impossible "to talk a man out of" his feelings. They are the most real and entrenched fact about him. And it is equally futile to argue whether or not the church should take stands where prejudices are involved. Those who believe that it should or should not speak out are very emotional about their convictions. The only time one is apt to hear a rational discussion is when all present are on the same side! But there is another level on which we can relate to one another when prejudices are involved. Each of us lives his life as the hero of a story. The themes that run through our story are never abstractions but embrace at best the fullness of our being. There is a certain integrity and intensity to the themes because they are a man's life story. You cannot dismiss a man as readily as an idea. I am suggesting that the level upon which we have some hope of "getting through" to one another is by telling our story. And that is what I propose to do now. This particular chapter centers upon my responses as a white man to colored men.

As you read do not be afraid to have your prejudices as well in full view. I want to lean my story against them.

I was raised in a community not unlike the ones from which many of you came. It was a white, Protestant, Republican ghetto. It was the kind of village that would have placed the one Negro in the congregation in the choir so that everyone would know they were broadminded! But no Negro can live there unless it is to serve a white man. For many years the only colored person I knew was the laundress. She was not given to much personal hygiene and compensated for the lack of it with cheap perfume. For that I silently condemned her, never thinking to censor the white landlord who provided no plumbing with his exorbitant rent. I was always polite to her, the kind of disinterested gentleman one learns to be at the country club to which we belonged. It did not concern me that she was in poor health, that her children had rejected her as old age made her presence less pleasurable, that the clothes she laundered for me she had never been able to afford for her family. She was just "a thing" that served me well. To this day when I see a Negro, my experiences with this woman affect my vision.

But before this memory blinds me to the person behind the dark skin, something else intrudes itself into the relationship. It is the vision of the God I have come to know in Christ. Here was One who knew well the differences between men. There were Gentiles and there were Jews, there were publicans and there were Pharisees, there were women of honor and women of the street, there were men of faith and men of doubt. But to Christ the differences between them made no difference in the way he loved them. He held them all together under one image of humanity. He claimed each as of unique worth by dying for them without discrimination. And because of the

way he cared for each, Paul could say, "There is neither
Jew nor Greek, there is neither slave nor free, there is
neither male nor female; for you are all one in Christ
Jesus" (Gal. 3:28). And while there are many Negroes
as well as whites who do not suit my pleasure, this event
of Christ comes between me and every person whom I
meet until my stereotypes and prejudices fade away.

Now this Christ makes a demand of me as he does of
every man who would call himself a Christian. And very
simply it is that I see each Negro as a person. He is not
essentially ignorant, essentially black, essentially limited in
potentiality, but essentially a human being—one who has
needs of love and forgiveness as I do, one who cares for
his children as I care for mine, one who works, struggles,
and dreams as I do.

And this is all the Negro is ultimately asking of us. He
doesn't want to marry your sister, her skin is too color-
less; he probably doesn't want to belong to your country
club, its activities would not appeal to him; he doesn't
want many of the "things" you and I feel are so essential,
to him they would be a burden. All he wants is personhood, the kind of personhood that can come only when
he is treated as a person. A friend of mine, a white pastor
in the South, went to call on Martin Luther King the
second day of King's imprisonment in Birmingham. He
was met by "Bull" Connors, the Director of Safety, who
prided himself on controlling the situation there. The pastor said, "I want to see Dr. Martin Luther King." Connors replied, "We have no *Dr*. Martin Luther King here."
Then my friend said, "I want to see Mr. Martin Luther
King." Connors replied, "We have no *Mr*. Martin Luther
King here." A third time my friend asked, "I want to see
Martin Luther King." And again Connors replied, "We
have no Martin Luther *King* here. All we got is a goddam

nigger." If you can escape this incident because it is from the South, listen to this voice from the North: "I'm the best friend the nigger's got. At Christmas I give the nigger at the country club a bottle of whiskey. When the son of the nigger who cleans our house needed a job, I got him one. I even have some niggers doing menial tasks in my business. I'm the best friend the nigger has—but he has his place, and it's serving his betters." Well, the Negro is tired of being a nigger taking the scraps from under the white man's table. He wants to be a person.

Now many of us who are sympathetic with the Negro cause are unsympathetic with the ways in which he is struggling to secure his rights. This is an issue upon which men of honor disagree. But I beg each of you, as I struggle myself, to reach behind our disagreements on method and understand that the Negro is tired of waiting for us to bestow upon him his rights as a person.

Listen to Martin Luther King: "For years now I have heard the word 'wait'! . . . This 'wait' has almost always meant 'never.' . . . We have waited for three hundred and forty years. . . . I guess it is easy for those who have never felt the stinging darts of segregation to say 'wait.' But when you have seen vicious mobs lynch your mothers and fathers at will and drown your sisters and brothers at whim; when you have seen hate-filled policemen curse, kick, brutalize, and even kill your black brother with impunity; when you see the vast majority of your twenty million Negro brothers smothering in an airtight cage of poverty in the midst of an affluent society; when you suddenly find your tongue twisted and your speech stammering as you seek to explain to your six-year-old daughter why she can't go to the public amusement park that has just been advertised on television, and see the tears welling up in her little eyes when she is told that

Funtown is closed to colored children, and see the depressing clouds of inferiority begin to form in her little mental sky; . . . when you are harried day and haunted night by the fact that you are a Negro, . . . then you will understand why we find it difficult to wait.'[53] There are many things the Negro is doing that I feel are unwise or imprudent. But when I think of how he has been abused as promises for a better tomorrow have rung their hollow hope, I only wonder that murder is not his daily intent. I'm afraid it would be mine.

But some by now are asking, "What can I do?" No one can answer that question for another. Each person must find that form in which he can give witness to his convictions. Yet there is one response on which all Christians can agree and which can be the format of every word and deed. And it is the recognition of who the Negro really is—whether he is rich or poor, clean or dirty, respectable or disreputable. He is the neighbor for whom I am responsible to God; in him I am to recognize Christ and the demands he has upon me. Jesus spoke of a day when there would be a separation between those faithful and those unfaithful to him. To those who were to inherit his Kingdom he said, "I was hungry and you gave me food, I was thirsty and you gave me drink, I was a stranger and you welcomed me, I was naked and you clothed me, I was sick and you visited me, I was in prison and you came to me" (Matt. 25:35-36). And when they asked when they had done this for him, he replied, "Truly, I say to you, as you did it to one of the least of these my brethren, you did it to me" (Matt. 25:40).

Some of you are familiar with the Glass family which J. D. Salinger has fictionalized in a continuing epic. All the seven children in this household are brilliant and their talents are displayed on a quiz program called "It's a Wise

Child." Seymour, the eldest, has told the others that they ought always to shine their shoes for "the Fat Lady" somewhere in the audience, an unknown woman who is lonely, unattractive, and suffering. Some years later Franny has an emotional breakdown, and her brother Zooey struggles to bring her out of it. Finally, invoking her to listen carefully, he discloses what he believes to be the secret of existence. *"There isn't anyone out there who isn't Seymour's Fat Lady. . . . [And] don't you know who that Fat Lady really is? . . . It's Christ Himself. Christ Himself, buddy."*[54]

Don't you know who the Negro is, the neighbor with darkened skin and troubled spirit? Don't you know who he really is? "It's Christ Himself. Christ Himself, buddy." Unless you come to the Negro aware of your sin and his need, you will never know the One called Christ. "I was hungry and you gave me food, . . . thirsty and you gave me drink, . . . a stranger and you welcomed me, . . . naked and you clothed me, . . . sick and you visited me, . . . in prison and you came to me." (Matt. 25:35-36.) It's Christ himself, buddy. And his face is black.

19

Black Power in Perspective

"To most whites," writes Stokely Carmichael, "black power seems to mean that the Mau Mau are coming to the suburbs at night."[55] In their nightmares the whites see their women raped by black avengers, their revered public officials castrated in the village square, and the orderly structures of government subverted by dupes of communism. What self-respecting suburbanite could sleep at night with the thought of Adam Clayton Powell directing the FBI, Cassius Clay presiding over the National Council of Churches, Dick Gregory serving as board chairman at General Motors, and a disciple of Malcolm X masterminding the local police force? While I suspect these fears and fantasies say more about white guilt than Negro aggression, they are as well a function of misunderstanding. Now that we have been through a rather torturous summer of rhetoric and rioting, it is even more difficult for white men to understand what black power at its best means to the Negro community. Perhaps that makes it even more imperative.

I

The most obvious thing to be said about black power is that it speaks to an identity crisis. I doubt that any of

us can fully understand the intensity with which the Negro
has perceived himself as a discolored and disfigured white
man. He has learned to be ashamed of being black, of
having a broad nose, thick lips, and kinky hair. His every
physical feature is experienced as a deviation from the
white norm. Characteristics that normally make a people
proud of themselves have led the Negro to embarrassment. And we ought not to underestimate the relationship
between one's body image and his sense of well-being.
How a person feels about his appearance is integral to
how he feels about himself in general. Sidney J. Jourard,
professor of psychology at the University of Florida, has
written that, "When one's body is disliked because of
deviations from norms . . . , evidence shows that anxiety, insecurity, and low self-esteem are regular corre-
lates."[56] Perhaps you have had this experience: You are
looking at yourself in a mirror before a date—your hair
won't stay in place, your nose appears bigger than you
ever imagined, and a blotch or two seems to disfigure
your whole appearance—before long you feel so awful
about yourself you don't even want to go out. The anal-
ogy may be trivial, but it does point up a dimension of
the identity crisis of the Negro. Having been led to perceive himself as discolored and disfigured, he feels dis-
pirited about himself.

We move more deeply into the problem when we
realize that nothing in our society reinforces his identity
as a Negro. Our culture is 90 percent white in color and
100 percent white in value structure. This means that
when the Negro makes it in our country it is because he
has distinguished himself on the white man's terms.
There is nothing distinctively Negro about Jackie Robinson's success in baseball, Ralph Bunche's success in
statesmanship, or Edward Brooke's success in politics.

We have reinforced them for being like us. We have done nothing to firm up the identity of the Negro as a Negro. Twenty years ago when the Negro preacher, Howard Thurman, was introduced on a college campus by its president who was a liberal in civil rights, he said, "Dr. Thurman has the face of a Negro but the soul of a white man." Even the more sensitive among us respond affirmatively when the Negro is like us.

Another dimension of the crisis emerges when we consider the identity that has been foisted on the Negro. Stokely Carmichael protests rather passionately, "From birth, black people have been told a pack of lies about themselves."[57] The behaviors of some have been impressed upon the race as characteristics and without any recognition of white responsibility. The Negro is told he is lazy by the white man who sits in a canvas chair watching him pick cotton for fourteen hours in the grueling Mississippi sun. He is told he is dishonest and untrustworthy by the white man who has made the minimum requirements of physical comfort inaccessible to him on any other terms. He is told that he is ignorant and therefore not ready for responsibility by the white man who has withheld adequate education. And he is told he is oversexed by the white man so insecure in his own sexuality that he has to prove his manliness by seducing the Negro's daughter, sister, and wife. If one is told enough lies about himself long enough, the lies begin to affect his self-image.

Do you begin to see why the identity crisis is so severe for the Negro? He has learned to dislike his body because it is disfigured and discolored by white norms. When he has been affirmed by the white community, it is because he has met white expectations. And then he has had foisted upon him characteristics the white man has induced. In our society there is nothing that enables him to appreciate or celebrate his uniqueness as a Negro.

It is into this gap that black power has moved and made a claim upon the Negro soul. Its success resides largely in its affirmations of the inherent qualities of Negritude. When Stokely Carmichael tells his audience, "Go home and tell your daughters they are beautiful," he is challenging them to accept themselves and be grateful for what they are. When he chastises them for using skin bleaches and hair straighteners and for their preference for lighter skin, he is attacking those acts of self-debasement which implicitly reaffirm white superiority. And when he calls upon them to reclaim their African history, to rejoice in their folkways and traditions, to exalt their cultural achievements in music and dance, he is denying every impulse to settle for a borrowed identity. And the message the Negro hears through the black power line is this: It's damn good to be a black. Believe in the qualities and possibilities of your race.

II

But the black power movement argues that it is not enough for the Negro to reclaim his identity. If the circumstances under which he lives are to be affected, he must participate aggressively in the power structures and strictures of the social order. He can no longer be a George Washington Carver, grateful for the little he has been given, or a Martin Luther King, protesting what he has been denied. He can only be effective in protecting his own interests if he has the political and economic strength to demand a hearing and to implement action. Humble appeals to the white conscience are both degrading and ineffective. It is by power he has been suppressed

and it is by power he will be liberated. And it is precisely
this which unnerves the white community. Power is a
dirty word in our vocabulary; the use of it is often perceived as a sign of weakness and moral bankruptcy. We
much prefer to think of morality, due process, and the
American way. But it just happens that each of these de-
pends upon a judicious use of power. We all protect our
interests with some form of pressure. The medical profession protects its rights through a powerful lobby in
Washington. The managements of industry stand together
as a power bloc to resist the demands of labor unions.
Students organize themselves into a form of government
through which they can exert influence upon the college.
Our nation asserts its own interests with assorted instruments of persuasion.

Might does not always make right, but it does protect
rights. And this is something the Negro has recognized.
When the white man holds all the power, the Negro can
only beg. But if the Negro gains his share of power, he
can negotiate from strength. Some would argue that this
is an extreme recourse. Those who say that fail to understand the problem. It is not discrimination, but "institutionalized racism." Discrimination means that I don't
want my daughter to paddle around in the same pool with
a colored girl. "Institutionalized racism" means that the
structures of society are ordered so as to macerate the
humanness of the Negro. When in Birmingham, Alabama,
"500 Negro babies die each year because of a lack of
proper food, shelter, and medical facilities, and thousands
more are destroyed and maimed"[58] in mind, body, and
psyche due to the poverty and deprivation of the ghetto,
that is "institutionalized racism." When the Negro does
not control the resources of that ghetto, does not make its
political decisions, does not participate in its law enforce-

ment, does not own its land, houses, and stores, but is at
the mercy of those who do, that is "institutionalized
racism." An appeal to the white conscience "to loosen
up the restrictions" is inadequate at best. The Negro must
be able to attack with strength the structures that have
suppressed him. It is a simple fact of our history that justice and decency emerge where there is a balance of
power, where each party can lead from strength. Majori-
ties never deal responsibly with minorities because they
ought to but because they have to. The use of power may
not convert the heart, but it can restrain the heartless; it
may not renovate values, but it can regulate behavior.

This is not "racism in reverse"; neither is it "black
nationalism." Black power represents the emergence of a
new generation of Negroes whose "goal is to organize
the black people of America into a militant, aggressive
political power bloc which can make just demands and
expect to have those demands met."[59] As such it is no
different from any other effort of a minority to establish
and protect its rights in competition with others. Obviously the privileges and priorities of many white people
will be challenged and threatened. Some will resent that.
But others will rejoice that we live in a democracy where
a minority can rise up and claim its rights.

III

Now I have been interpreting black power as a movement to secure the Negro in his identity and to mobilize
the race as a force in the social order. In other words, it
is a sign that the Negro is coming into his possibilities,
emerging from infantile dependency toward a maturity in
which he can say with tongue in cheek, "Some of my best
friends are white." He is determined to ensure that the

future will not be a cruel repetition of the past. This
phenomenon resembles an event in the New Testament
(Luke 5:17-26). A small group of men set before Jesus
a paralytic whom they believed he could heal. Without so
much as taking the man's pulse, Jesus said, "Man, your
sins are forgiven you." And then without waiting for a
response he thrust an imperative into his existence: " 'I
say to you, rise, take up your bed and go home.' And immediately he rose before them, and took up that on which
he lay, and went home, glorifying God." Now let's reword
the story. One who has been immobilized by his past is
set before Jesus with the expectation that he can be freed
of it. Jesus looks at him and says: "Your past no longer
limits you. You are free to come into your own. Go to
it." And the paralytic trusted his freedom and acted upon
it. He went his own way, grateful only to God. That is
what is happening to the American Negro. The words of
life about his possibilities as a human being have come to
him, and he believes them. He is going to live like a man,
in his own way. In the face of that the Christian can only
rejoice.

20

A Nightmare in November

John F. Kennedy had gone to Texas to heal a breach within his party and gain support for his Administration. On the morning of November 22, 1963, his motorcade made its way toward the heart of Dallas. The presence of the vigorous young leader provoked a thunderous response. It hardly seemed possible that three years earlier this city had cast its ballot for his opponent. The wife of Governor Connally looked up admiringly and said, "Mr. President, they love you here." At 12:30 P.M. the motorcade turned onto Elm Street and at a speed of eleven miles per hour headed toward the Trade Mart where Mr. Kennedy was to speak. Seconds later bullets slit the air, and the President's hands reflexed to his neck. He lurched forward only to be struck in the back of the head. Mrs. Kennedy, holding her husband in her arms, was heard to say: "Oh, my God, they have shot my husband. I love you, Jack."

It was a typical Friday in most communities. Work was almost over and thoughts of the weekend had set in. Then across the land individuals in dazed confusion darted into this gathering and that with the news that the President had been shot. "Sure he has, do you know any more jokes," some responded. Then most gathered before the television. Young men who moments before had laughed and clowned now held their heads as if to keep them from exploding. Young women so composed and confident moments before now sobbed—some silently, others audibly. Then the word came, breaking the insufferable suspense: "President John F. Kennedy is dead. The last rites were administered by a priest at 1:00 P.M." That night many gathered in churches, still hoping it was not true, that someone would say, "Wake up now, it's a new day." It was a nightmare in November, but when we awoke it was not over. The hurt dug deeper and reached the depths for many of us when we saw little John salute his father's casket.

History will record it as the story of Lee Oswald and John Kennedy. The disturbed and frustrated man who in cowardly scheme slew an able leader. The Bible tells the same story; there it's of Cain and Abel, Cain a tiller of the soil and Abel a keeper of sheep (Gen. 4:1-16). As became the custom in Israel, each brought to the altar of God an offering from the firstfruits of his labor. For reasons perhaps never to be known, the sacrifice of Abel was accepted, that of Cain rejected. When the rebuke became more than he could bear, Cain said to his brother, "Let us go out to the field." Abel must have been touched that his brother coveted time alone with him, but the touch was lethal. "Cain rose up against his brother Abel, and killed him." He had done it out of the sight of men but not of God. And there came from the Lord a question that pierced his privacy: "Where is Abel your brother?" With the grace of a guiltless man Cain replied, "I do not know; am I my brother's keeper?" The Lord did not relent: "What have you done? The voice of your brother's blood is crying to me from the ground." For his offense Cain is told, "You shall be a fugitive and

a wanderer on the earth." "Then Cain went away from
the presence of the LORD, and dwelt in the land of Nod,
east of Eden."

Let's wrestle with that a moment. In literal translation
the land of Nod is the place of restlessness and wandering, of futile strife and senseless deed. It's the place of
man after the fall, after he's said in one way or another
he'll take his life with himself at the center. It's where we
meet now—not in joyous and grace-full encounter—but
where a lethal blow marks our way with one another.
The land of Nod is Hiroshima, New York, Israel, Vietnam, Dallas, Birmingham. It's the place of homelessness
and no security. And Cain is the main character in the
drama, the prototype of the abysmal depths in man.

The mark of Cain is on Lee Oswald. Here was one
whose home was no home—a father who had not fathered
him, another father whom he never knew, a mother too
obsessed with her own needs to meet his. She claims he
was a good boy, but one suspects she never knew her
son. He was never more homeless than at home. In time
he sought a place of glory in the Marine Corps. The
dashing uniform and the martial music must have given
him moments of exhilaration. But back in the barracks
he was alone and frightened, withdrawn into himself.
After that there was the excitement of an ideology, a place
under the sun in Marxist equalitarianism. Leaving behind
a homeless home, he escaped into the incarnation of his
dream. But even in Russia he was a fugitive and a
wanderer. With borrowed money he returned to the land
of his birth and sought himself in a crusade. The revolu-
tion in Cuba caught his imagination and in the midst of
senseless and unresponsive crowds he distributed propa-

ganda. Yet there was no home or security in that. We will never know what desperate urge led him with a cheap mail-order rifle to the sixth floor of a warehouse, there to sight a President in his range finder, there to pull a trigger and end a life. This time, not in a field far from the sight of men but in an exuberant crowd. "Cain rose up against his brother Abel, and killed him" (Gen. 4:8).

The mark of Cain is upon us as well and the land of Nod our habitation. Who among us has not found his world a place of no security and fulfillment, who among us has not felt himself to be a fugitive in a land forever strange?—running from dream to disillusionment, from responsibility to shelter, seeking security in the passing moment and feeling cheated by it, drawing everything up into ourselves until we have a centerless center. We seek a homeland in romance, but it becomes exploitation as a kiss echoes in an empty heart. We give ourselves to tasks but they become vacuous and barren. We find meaning for a moment but it eludes our grasp. Then our land of Nod becomes the stage upon which we bleed from the wounds of Cain. But we have not slain our brother; or have we? Perhaps our slaughterers are more respectable. Sometimes the lethal deed is a word withheld from a person who is in need or a word spoken as a sword piercing the personality of another. Sometimes the lethal deed is indifference—gracious unconcern with the vital issues of the day in which the lives of others are tortured and distorted. Sometimes the lethal deed is moral insensitivity, the determination to make oneself the measure of all actions. It's the land of Nod—and we are Cain. It's the game of life—but the rules are unfair, the victory withheld, the dreams forever nightmares. And the best we do is curse the darkness or live by lights that fade. That's our world, is it not?

II

But something has happened. The abysmal depths of what we are and the life we live have been illumined. The Bible is richly figurative and one of its images for the presence of God is light. The psalmist sings of it: "The LORD is my light and my salvation; whom shall I fear?" (Ps. 27:1). Micah speaks of it in confidence: "When I sit in darkness, the LORD will be a light to me" (Micah 7:8). Isaiah witnesses to its eternity: "The LORD will be your everlasting light" (Isa. 60:20). And the Gospel of John celebrates its having come in Christ: "In him was life, and the life was the light of men. The light shines in the darkness, and the darkness has not overcome it" (John 1:4-5). It's all the Bible's way of saying that the abyss within and around us has been invaded and illumined.

But can we say that *we* have seen the light, even a faint flicker or a shadow? Some say not, and with good reason. Ancient creed and perfunctory ritual have extinguished it. The pious have held it to themselves until they have smothered it. The church has buried it in bazaars and saccharine Sunday schools. The pulpit has betrayed it with irrelevance and "gossip about God." And with all that, the torturous events of history—Hiroshima, Dallas, Birmingham—have confirmed us in the lightless life. Perhaps the only light we have seen or come to expect is that attending nuclear explosions. And that's but another form of darkness. What happened to the light of which Scripture speaks?

Nothing, really; we simply have not learned to recognize it, call it by name, or trust its eternal source. The light seldom presents itself in clear and unmistakable form; by its very nature it never calls attention to itself, that would be idolatry. But light does shine through cracks in the walls of ordinary experience. Some of us saw it in Lou Marsh, about whom you may have read. He had been a divinity student for whom studies lost their meaning. Interrupting his degree program at Yale, Lou Marsh sought to find himself in the world of East Harlem. Assigned by the New York City Youth Board to work with juvenile gangs, he infiltrated and gained the confidence of one that called itself "The Untouchables." One night a "rumble" was scheduled between them and "The Playboys," a rival gang. Lou mediated and it was called off. But some of their "alumni" resented the fact that violence had been averted, that conflict was not to be resolved in strife. On January 9, 1963, four of them beat Lou Marsh to death. The life went out of his body, but the light of his life shown on the dark streets of Harlem. When Howard Moody preached at his funeral hundreds of youngsters who had never been inside a church before, many who had never graced a shirt and tie, were there. It was their way of acknowledging that there had been in their midst one with a depth of humanness they had not known before. The light shown in the darkness and the darkness could not overcome it, even in death.

That's exceptional you say, nothing in which I might be involved. Perhaps so. But that same light has shown in you and among those you know. The forms may have been more respectable, but the depth of humanness no less intense and real. There are moments in which men meet each other in authentic relationships and grasp what love can mean. There are moments in which individuals rise above the crowd and take a stand for honor and integrity. There are moments in which persons have faced the abysmal depth of their existence, where life seemed not worth living and each day a burden beyond bearing, yet came out with a grasp on what was real within themselves. There are moments in which neighbors broke through the walls of insensitivity and prejudice and responded to the needs of another. There are moments in which churchmen contended with the innocuous expressions of religion, resisted false piety and moralistic facade, and dug beneath the surface to be grounded in something Ultimate. Then the light shown in the darkness, and the darkness could not overcome it.

That light was not ignited by men, nor did it burn on human striving. It was inflamed, though often we know it not, by another light, one a cross could not extinguish. Then men, for a moment at least, were children of light, humanized and humanizing in an inhuman darkness. Then they participated in the Ground of their Being, even as it is known in Jesus who is the Christ. "In him was life, and the life was the light of men." (John 1:4.)

21

The Covenant of Intimacy

It may not appear to square with our firsthand experience but the fact remains that one in four marriages ends in divorce. There is, of course, a healthy sign in that statistic. Increasingly men and women who do not have "the makings of a marriage" are facing up to that and taking leave of a futile state of respectability. At the same time it raises for all of us who stand within the marriage commitment, or who aspire to it, the question of durability. We need to have before us the contours of a responsible and creative marriage, that which remains after much of the glamour and excitement has worn off. Recently my six-year-old daughter set the issue before us when she viewed for the first time a photograph of her mother in her wedding gown. She backed off for a moment and then exclaimed, "Gee, Dad, Mother was a princess when you married her!" I knew what she meant. Her mother sensed the communication going on between us and chimed in, "In those days, Sara, your father was a dashing figure too." Honesty demands the confession that she was the only woman who thought so!

What light does the Christian faith shed on the marriage relationship? How shall we conceive the covenant of intimacy between a man and a woman? What is the enduring dimension when dad is no longer perceived as dashing and mother as a princess?

I

Now the covenant of intimacy is based upon a promise within a premise. That premise is set before us in the story of creation (Gen. 2:18-25). God is reported to have done his work each day and then backed off and said, "It is good, it is very good." But on the sixth day he determined that it was not good enough. There was night and there was day, there was water and there was land, there were birds of the air and beasts of the field. And then there was Adam, just Adam. "It is not good that the man should be alone," God discovered; "I will make him a helper fit for him." There needed to be another with whom Adam could have a unique relationship. "So the LORD God caused a deep sleep to fall upon the man, and while he slept took one of his ribs . . . and the rib the LORD God had taken from the man he made into a woman and brought her to the man." And Adam responded, "This at last is bone of my bones and flesh of my flesh." Here in poetic narrative is the premise: that God has provided man and woman for each other. Emil Brunner calls it "the order creation," the divine gift offered as the possibility of fulfillment.

But to this premise a man and a woman are invited to bring a promise. Their relationship is not based on feelings of affection, they wain from time to time; it is not based on romantic love, that scarcely lasts beyond youth; it is not based on their mutual needs, these lead to exploitation; and it is not based on interests or diversions they have in common, they change with the years. Marriage is rooted in the promises a man and a woman make to each other. Love is not a feeling, it is an intention. The wedding service sets this forth. The minister only asks one thing of each and it is a declaration of intention. "John, *wilt* thou have this Woman to be thy wife, and *wilt* thou pledge thy troth to her, in all love and honor, in all duty and service, in all faith and tenderness, to live with her, and cherish her, according to the ordinance of God in the holy bond of marriage?" And he is required to respond, as she is later, "I *will*." The service does not celebrate their feelings, explore their compatability, or identify their goals in life. It centers on the promise of self to self.

Some of you may be familiar with Thornton Wilder's play *The Skin of Our Teeth*. Near the end Mrs. Antrobus calls up before her wayward husband the real basis of their marriage. "I didn't marry you because you were perfect. I didn't even marry you because I loved you. I married you because you gave me a promise." Taking off her wedding band and examining it, she continues: "That promise made up for your faults. And the promise I gave you made up for mine. Two imperfect people got married and it was that promise that made the marriage."[60]

I suspect that this is one of the most important things that those of us who are married need to be reminded of and that needs to be held up before those who anticipate this relationship. There are times when the feelings of affection will not be strong, when their interests will part like the Nile, and when their presence to each other will be distorted by a hate which is love gone astray. Then each can only lay claim to the words, "I promised," within the premise that God appointed man and woman for each other, "I promised myself to this woman."

II

When we return to the creation story we see that the covenant of intimacy involves an act of presentation as well. After God had made Eve from the rib of Adam, he offered them to each other. In effect he said: "Here she is, Adam; here he is, Eve. How are you going to relate to each other?" The Biblical writer answers the question: "Therefore a man leaves his father and his mother and cleaves to his wife, and they become one flesh" (Gen. 2:24). On one level the writer is merely trying to explain the universal instinct of man and woman for each other. Because Eve was made from the rib of Adam, it is a return of the separated into union. But more importantly, the author is contending that there is the possibility of an intimacy between a man and a woman which even exceeds the bond between parent and child. They can present themselves to each other with an intensity and an integrity that is nowhere exceeded. Marriage is the place where you need not fear to be fully known, to give yourself away. Here one can dare to share himself in trust.

Several years ago Richard Aldrich wrote a biographical tribute to his actress wife, Gertrude Lawrence. "As an actress," he wrote, "Gertrude Lawrence is a beloved figure to millions. Bewitching and elusive as a moonbeam, she flitted from the terrace of the Carleton at Cannes to a millionaire's yacht off Palm Beach, enchanting her audiences, rekindling in their hearts something which in too many of us dims and flickers out after first youth. But Mrs. A. is a woman who was known slightly to not more than a dozen persons. And fully, intimately to only one —myself."[61] Only in the context of marriage where promises have been exchanged can one expose himself so boldly. Only there can one appoint another guardian of his secrets.

When this happens within a covenant, the dominant experience is of freedom. We all carry with us through life a bundle of knowledge and feelings about ourselves. There are instincts and passions of which we are ashamed; there are dreams too unreal to be made public; there are talents we have not had courage to express; there are moods we cannot erase; there are features of personality and body we cannot openly share. What we know of ourselves is more than we can live with by ourselves. But all this can be known and accepted by one who has promised himself to us. In marriage I can accept the light and dark sides of myself because there is another who affirms me just as I am. I am free of myself when in many different ways each day there is a mate who says, "I know what you are like, and it doesn't make any difference."

III

But then in the context of the promise and the presentation of self to self, the Biblical faith identifies a Presence. The Jewish theologian Martin Buber goes to the heart of this when he writes, "He who loves a woman, and brings her life to present realization in his, is able to look in the Thou of her eyes into the beam of the Eternal Thou."[62] The mystery and majesty of marriage is its transparency to God. He is seldom so real as in the unitive bond between two persons whose love for each other is a response to the love God has for both of them. Several years ago I was talking with a senior who acknowledged that throughout college he had been indifferent to the Christian faith. But then he added, "You know, I'm going to be married this summer and I need to examine my relationship with God." Here was the recognition that the covenant into which he was entering required him to come to terms with more than the lady of his choice. The closest most of us ever come to God is in the middle of our confrontation with the one we love. When a man and a woman stand before each other in their fullness they are susceptible to an Eternal Thou.

The significance of this Presence is that it enables us to understand the kind of love required of them. Paul sets before us the claim to receive one another as Christ has received us. The style of love evidenced in Christ is a model for the love between a man and a woman. And the New Testament is resplendent with pictures of that Love. It looks like being utterly honest with one another. There's a woman at the well claiming she had no husband, and Jesus saying, "Come on now, you have had five." It looks like accepting someone when he least deserves it. There's the despised tax collector, and Jesus motioning him down from the tree saying, "Zacchaeus, I'm going to have dinner in your home." It looks like concern for the physical needs of another. There's Jesus with the five thousand listening to him to the point of hunger and his bidding the multitude to share the fishes and the loaves. It looks like a willingness to forgive even one who has offended you most deeply. There's Jesus beholding his persecutors and saying, "Father, forgive them" (Luke 23:34). It looks like going all the way with another, holding nothing back for oneself. There's Jesus on the cross sacrificing himself in affirmation of all men. The Bible is not first concerned with the love you can achieve but the love you have received. Christ is in the midst of a marriage enabling us to implement the love with which he loves us. That ultimately is its durability.

Notes

1. Thomas J. J. Altizer and William Hamilton, *Radical Theology and the Death of God* (The Bobbs-Merrill Company, Inc., 1966), p. x.

2. William Hamilton, "The Death of God Theology," *The Christian Scholar,* Spring, 1965, p. 40.

3. William Hamilton, "The Shape of a Radical Theology," *The Christian Century,* October 6, 1965, p. 1221

4. Martin Noth, *Exodus, A Commentary,* tr. by J. S. Bowden (The Westminster Press, 1962), p. 45.

5. Harry H. Kruener, unpublished Baccalaureate Address at Denison University, June, 1965.

6. Tennessee Williams, *Sweet Bird of Youth* (New Directions, 1959), Act II, Scene 3.

7. Quoted in Walter Leibrecht (ed.), *Religion and Culture* (Harper & Brothers, 1959), p. 100.

8. Alan Richardson, *Science, History and Faith* (London: Oxford University Press, 1950), p. 2.

9. Dietrich Bonhoeffer, *Prisoner for God* (The Macmillan Company, 1957), p. 128.

10. Quoted by Paul Elmen, *The Restoration of Meaning to Contemporary Life* (Doubleday & Company, Inc., 1958), p. 150.

11. Quoted by Nathan A. Scott, Jr., *Modern Literature and the Religious Frontier* (Harper & Brothers, 1958), p. 74.

12. Richard L. Rubenstein, *After Auschwitz* (The Bobbs-Merrill Company, Inc., 1966), p. 151.

13. Harvey Cox, *The Secular City* (The Macmillan Company, 1965), p. 262.

14. Robert W. Spike, *To Be a Man* (Association Press, 1961), p. 123.

15. Archibald MacLeish, *J.B.* (Houghton Mifflin Company, 1956), p. 93.

16. *Ibid.,* p. 153.

17. Friedrich Nietzsche, *Thus Spake Zarathustra,* Part IV, Ch. 67 (Modern Library, Inc., 1954), pp. 264-267.

18. Edward Albee, *Who's Afraid of Virginia Woolf?* (Atheneum Publishers, 1962), p. 50. Copyright © 1962 by Edward Albee.

19. *Ibid.,* pp. 84-85.

20. *Ibid.,* p. 142.

21. *Ibid.,* p. 145.

22. *Ibid.,* pp. 146-147.

23. *Ibid.,* pp. 229-233.

24. *Ibid.,* pp. 239-241.

25. John Killinger, *The Thickness of Glory* (Abingdon Press, 1964), pp. 91-92.

26. Quoted in Carl Michalson, *Faith for Personal Crises* (Charles Scribner's Sons, 1958), p. 84.

27. Quoted by Will Herberg in *Sermons to Intellectuals,* ed. by Franklin H. Littell (The Macmillan Company, 1963), p. 29.

28. Herbert Butterfield, *Christianity and History* (Charles Scribner's Sons, 1950), p. 146.

29. Frederico Fellini, *La Dolce Vita* (Ballantine Books, Inc., 1961), pp. 1-2.

30. Quoted in Paul M. van Buren, *The Secular Meaning of the Gospel* (The Macmillan Company, 1963), p. 1.

31. Karl Barth, *Church Dogmatics* I/2 (Edinburgh: T. & T. Clark, 1956), pp. 299-300.

32. Samuel H. Miller, *The Dilemma of Modern Belief* (Harper & Row, Publishers, Inc., 1963), p. 69.

33. Paul Tillich, *The Shaking of the Foundations* (Charles Scribner's Sons, 1948), pp. 106-107.

34. Bonhoeffer, *Prisoner for God,* p. 128.

35. Quoted in *Time,* March 9, 1962, p. 53.

36. Albert Camus, *The Fall* (Alfred A. Knopf, Inc., 1957), p. 73.

37. Jean-Paul Sartre, *No Exit and Three Other Plays* (Vintage Books, Inc., 1957), p. 47.

38. John A. T. Robinson, *Honest to God* (The Westminster Press, 1963), p. 99.

39. Barth, *Church Dogmatics* I/2, pp. 299-300.

40. Paul Tillich, *The New Being* (Charles Scribner's Sons, 1955), pp. 17-18.

41. *Ibid.*, p. 24.

42. John A. T. Robinson, *The New Reformation?* (The Westminster Press, 1965), p. 128.

43. Albert Camus, *The Plague* (Alfred A. Knopf, Inc., 1948), p. 231.

44. Joseph Sittler, *The Structure of Christian Ethics* (Louisiana State University Press, 1958), p. 50.

45. Paul Tillich, *Morality and Beyond* (Harper & Row, Publishers, Inc., 1963), p. 44.

46. Quoted in Kingsley Amis, *The James Bond Dossier* (The New American Library of World Literature, Inc., 1965), p. 37.

47. Quoted by Ann S. Boyd, "James Bond: Modern-Day Dragonslayer," *The Christian Century,* May 19, 1965.

48. T. S. Eliot, "The Hollow Men," *The Complete Poems and Plays* (Harcourt, Brace & Company, Inc., 1934), p. 56.

49. Ian Fleming, *Goldfinger* (The New American Library of World Literature, Inc., 1959), p. 7. © 1959 by Glidrose Productions Ltd. Used by permission.

50. Arthur Miller, *The Misfits* (The Viking Press, Inc., 1957), pp. 6-7. Copyright © 1957, 1961 by Arthur Miller. Used by permission.

51. Earl A. Loomis, Jr., *The Self in Pilgrimage* (Harper & Brothers, 1960), pp. 56-57.

52. Gerhard von Rad, *Genesis: A Commentary* (The Westminster Press, 1961), p. 56.

53. Martin Luther King, "Letter from a Birmingham Prison."

54. J. D. Salinger, *Franny and Zooey* (London: William Heinemann, Ltd., 1955), p. 200.

55. Stokely Carmichael, "What We Want," *The New York Review,* September 22, 1966.

56. Sidney M. Jourard, *The Transparent Self* (D. Van Nostrand Company, Inc., 1964), p. 91.

57. Carmichael, "What We Want."

58. Stokely Carmichael, "Toward Black Liberation" (Student Nonviolent Coordinating Committee, 1966).

59. Richard Newman, "The Black Power Resolution," a sermon preached in Marsh Chapel, Boston University, January 15, 1967.

60. Quoted in Charles R. Stinnette, *Grace and the Searching of Our Heart* (Association Press, 1962), p. 118.

61. Quoted in John Charles Wynn, *Pastoral Ministry to Families* (The Westminster Press, 1962), p. 132.

62. *Ibid.*, p. 130.